STANDING

IN YOUR

OWN WAY

Standing in Your Own Way

■

Talks on the Nature of Ego

Anthony Damiani

PUBLISHED FOR THE PAUL BRUNTON
PHILOSOPHIC FOUNDATION BY

Larson Publications

International Standard Book Number: 0-943914-60-4
Library of Congress Catalog Card Number: 92-74546

Published for the
Paul Brunton Philosophic Foundation by
Larson Publications
4936 State Route 414
Burdett, New York 14818

98 97 96 95 94 93 92
10 9 8 7 6 5 4 3 2 1

CONTENTS

FOREWORD

This invigorating book cuts through the fog of clichés and propaganda that obscures the most immediate—and most painfully misunderstood—issue of traditional teachings about individuation and self-realization. "New age" teachings generally try to sidestep this issue altogether. Individual doctrines within the traditional fold tend to overemphasize certain aspects of it at the expense of others. In stark contrast, this book offers a uniquely wholesome notion of the ego's nature and the range it encompasses.

Anthony Damiani was deeply versed in traditional thought, and acutely aware of the broad variety of meanings given the word "ego" in contemporary psychology. His focus in the classes on which this book is based, however, was very specific: *what a spiritual seeker needs to know about the nuts and bolts of the work at hand.* A few remarks about the background of the classes will provide a helpful context for the discussions presented here.

In September of 1981, Anthony received the originals of extensive notebooks his teacher Paul Brunton (PB) had reserved for posthumous publication. Having worked independently of PB for many years, he was astounded by the breadth and clarity of these writings and spent all his free time for the next year reading them. By August of 1982 he had concluded that PB's notes on the ego, in particular, would be of extraordinary value to his own students.

Anthony gave two series of classes on this subject; the first in 1982; the second in 1984.

In the first cycle of classes, Anthony introduced PB's notes on the ego somewhat randomly. PB himself had not organized them into a point-by-point order in his notebooks, and Anthony was not ready to try to structure them into one. Instead, he recommended that his students read and discuss each notebook entry ("para") as if it stood alone. He was strongly opposed to attempts to organize the material until it had first been encountered in this way.

His reason for this was simple. In most of us, the intellect that would attempt the organizing is itself a tool in service of the ego's presuppositions; and the ego has a vested interest in not being seen clearly. Thus in the beginning we were virtually guaranteed of making "connections" that would take us off track rather than deeper into PB's individual remarks.

On a typical class night, at least sixty students would gather in one large room at Wisdom's Goldenrod. Several paras would be read at the beginning, students would start asking questions, and then more paras would be read and discussed. In the first cycle, Anthony encouraged a good deal of student discussion before offering his own views.

In the second cycle, however, Anthony knew he had little time to live. Though physically weak and often short of breath, he was warmly intimate and in excellent humor. But feeling the shortage of time, he was calmly insistent on getting to the heart of this matter with the breath left in him. He returned selectively to many of the most important notes, and several of them were discussed a number of times in different classes. In general, he still restricted himself to a careful elaboration of one para at a time. But occasionally he used one as a stepping-off point from which to share his own synthetic understanding and overview of the material. One month after giving his last class on the ego notes, and just days after meeting with his dear friend the Dalai Lama in Middlebury, Vermont, he died peacefully in his home in Valois, New York.

Since then, the most important sections of the writings PB reserved for posthumous publication have been published. Most are in the sixteen-volume series entitled *The Notebooks of Paul Brunton*; some are in the collection of essays entitled *Essays on the Quest*. References within the present book to writings in the *Notebooks* series are identified by volume number, category, chapter, and entry number. V6, 8:1.135, for example, means volume 6, category 8, chapter 1, entry 135.

Standing in Your Own Way is structured thematically, rather than according to the historical sequence of the classes themselves. With only two exceptions that will be obvious to readers, we have gathered together from various classes the key points of dialogue on notebook entries that were discussed more than once. As such, this book serves a double purpose.

On one hand, it stands on its own as a uniquely powerful and valuable contribution to the literature of spiritual realization. On the other, it provides a background and overview that will be of great service to readers of volume six in *The Notebooks of Paul Brunton* (the volume entitled *The Ego/From Birth to Rebirth*). The paras Anthony elucidates in *Standing in Your Own Way*—while including most of PB's key ideas on the ego—are but a small percentage of the much larger body of material to be found in volume six of the *Notebooks* series.

We hope that this book will be as helpful to its readers as the information it contains has been to those who attended the inspiring classes on which it is based. Readers who would like to know more about Anthony Damiani are directed to the biographical sketch in our earlier publication of his work on meditation and mentalism, entitled *Looking into Mind* (Larson, 1990).

Editors, Wisdom's Goldenrod
October 1992

THIS NARROW fragment of consciousness which is the person that I am hides the great secret of life at its core.

(v6, 8:1.111)

THE EGO's consciousness is a vastly reduced, immeasurably weakened echo of the Overself-Consciousness. It is always changing and dissipates in the end whereas the Other is ever the same and undying. But the ego is drawn out of the Other and must return to it, so the link is there. What is more, the possibility of returning voluntarily and deliberately is also there.

(v6, 8:1.135)

CHAPTER ONE

RECOGNIZING THE PROBLEM

THE EGO is always in hiding and often in disguise. It is
a cunning creature, never showing its own face, so that
even the man who wants to destroy its rule is easily
tricked into attacking everything else but the ego!
Therefore, the first (as well as the final) essential piece
of knowledge needed to track it down to its secret lair
is how to recognize and identify it.   (v6, 8:4.391)

ANTHONY: Listen to that. You've first got to know what the
ego is, and what you're looking for. That's why this knowledge
is so important. Once you're seriously on the quest, that's going to be your preoccupation. Long or short path or combination, it doesn't matter. You've got to know what it is you're
dealing with. So this knowledge is absolutely vital. Anybody
who talks about the non-existence of the ego, or glorifies it, or
says it's illusory, all that is beside the point.

    HS: But I don't really see how gaining information about
the deeper part of the ego is necessarily spiritual.

    ANTHONY: You don't think it would be spiritual for you to
know something about your ego?

    HS: Not necessarily, no.

ANTHONY: In that case then you would have to suffer the consequences of whatever it desired, right? You'd go around serving it all the time. Would you want to do that?

HS: But is knowing the deeper aspect of one's personal self spiritual, or concordant with knowledge of the higher?

ANTHONY: Yes, because if you try practicing the higher practices, the ego will come in and show you exactly how to accommodate it. If you're going to get on the quest, you can't be a nincompoop for too long. It hurts. After a while it becomes painful. After a while it becomes excruciating. So to know something about the devious ways the ego operates—its strategies, its tremendous comprehension of how to keep you always under its power—there's some spiritual value in that. These are things we have to know.

Put the metaphysical discussions aside. Let's stick to the brutality, the reality that we are.

AH: If you knew some of the deeper aspects of this ego, you might know a deep enough aspect to realize that it has a kind of tenuous existence.

ANTHONY: Don't kid yourself. Don't come to me from the point of view that the ego doesn't exist, because it's been around as long as the Overself[1] has been projecting itself, manifesting itself through some kind of a life. The residue of all that living becomes a tendency which you're going to find is perhaps not a permanent entity, but good enough to drive you up a wall for the next indefinite number of incarnations. If you think you're going to enter into the arena of spiritual struggle and quest without having a real good idea of what's going on with your ego, you're in for trouble.

AH: It's sometimes spoken of as empty.

ANTHONY: I know. As soon as you say the *ego* is "empty" then you're in for it. I don't think you understand why I regard any talk like that as utterly futile and even esoterically stupid. I don't care who says it.

Anyone who thinks he's going to outwit his ego is in for a real rough time. That's why I don't like to call it empty. I like to think of it as a real fire-breathing dragon. If I come within a few feet of that breath, I get intoxicated.

AH: What does it mean, then, to understand the deeper aspects of the ego, the more surreptitious and subterranean aspects of it?

ANTHONY: That's what it means.

AH: Do we become more and more fearful of it?

ANTHONY: No. Let me remind you of what PB[2] is saying, so you can have respect for your enemy and know who it is and perhaps even be aware of the way it's going to come at you—even in the highest states, including all the way up to the void. Because in the void it can't hide. You can't have thought there, so it can't hide there; it gets exposed. But everywhere else it goes up with you, every step of the way. So we have to discuss it, we have to try to understand it.

AH: So when we sit down to meditate we should look for the ego?

ANTHONY: No, when you sit down to meditate, you are doing something else. You are trying to develop that necessary introversion by which and through which you can become aware of the ego.

As we read and discuss these quotes, you'll get a comprehensive picture of what the ego is in terms of its lowest and its highest, the range that it encompasses. On one hand, it's a projection or a manifestation of the Overself. But on the other hand, you can misidentify yourself with the ego and get lost in the net or the web of illusion that it spins out for you.

So you have to plant yourself firmly in the middle of everything PB says about the ego and go about systematically exploring what he means by it: metaphysically, ontologically, epistemologically, psychologically. You need to see all these various aspects that it has—instead of assuming that you know it just because you feel nice and warm here and there, now and then. Anything that we can understand about it will be to our benefit.

LR: Given a specific situation . . .

ANTHONY: Before we worry about a specific situation that may arise, I would suggest that we try to get, as much as we can, an overall comprehensive grasp of the many facets that the ego has. Then you can worry about applying it to any contingent situation. First get this general overall framework that PB is delivering to you so that at least you become aware. Even that's going to be quite insignificant when it starts its attacks.

JB: Insofar as the ego has a conception of a real self, there's some unconscious awareness of the existence of a reality.

ANTHONY: No. No. No. The ego is interested in one thing, and that is preserving itself. It has no awareness of the higher consciousness. It would get *lost* if there was a higher consciousness. In *nirvikalpa*,[3] it is suppressed, it isn't there. Could you understand this?

Think of the Overself constantly manifesting throughout eons of time, and that you came up from the stone, through the plant, through the animal, and into the human species, and that in all this process of manifestation, the ego was concerned with one thing, preserving itself. And then if you conceive of that tendency—which is only a thought but strong enough to strangle us every moment of the day—if you conceive of that tendency, then you tell me that tendency knows the higher Awareness? Of course not. The only thing it knows is that it must preserve intact that tendency to go on being what it is.

RG: You're saying that the tendency itself becomes the "self" because that's all it knows?

ANTHONY: Yes, but that self certainly should not be confused with Self. Now if you notice, the ego does that all the time, to the class, to us, to each and every individual here. Every moment of the day.

AH: The Buddhists point out that the ego has no permanence, that wherever you look for it, you can't find it.

ANTHONY: But it's strangling you every moment! It doesn't matter that I can't find it.

HS: How would you examine this strangling?

ANTHONY: That's what we're doing here. We're trying to expose its secret work.

HS: And the way to do it is?

ANTHONY: Well, let a master tell you about it.

IT IS NOT so much a matter of destroying the ego as of balancing it with the Overself, for its need of development must be recognized. Such an act will not give it equal power but put it in its proper place, as a child's individuality needs to be balanced with its parents'.

(v6, 8:1.179)

THE EGO is a part of the divine order of existence. It must emerge, grow, enslave, and finally be enslaved.

(v6, 8:1.165)

HS: How do you understand that? The ego is part of the *divine* order of existence.

ANTHONY: Well, it's part of the World-Idea, part of the divine order of things—the Divine Idea of the World. It's going to have to grow, it's going to have to develop, refine itself, dominate the soul, and then in turn be dominated by the soul.

The World-Idea is constantly being evolved until it approaches the goal that the Idea's trying to achieve. And since the ego is an idea or part of the Idea, the Universal Idea, the World-Idea, it too has to go through that improvement and evolution. As the world, so to speak, evolves closer and closer to the paradigms that have been set for it, so the egos within that world have to evolve.

This offers a much more complete and wholesome notion of what the ego is, rather than the limited perspectives that say either it doesn't exist or it's not real or it's this, that, or the other. PB is building up a tremendous, holistic view of what the ego is, what its role is, what it's like, what's supposed to happen. When he gets finished with all the remarks he makes on the ego, you come away with a balanced idea of what it's all about, instead of these naïve notions—it doesn't exist, it does exist, this that and the other thing—which are really clichés and propaganda that have nothing to do with the issue.

BS: It depends on the vantage point you're taking.

ANTHONY: Well, that's what you want. You want a vantage point to see what it's all about instead of being deluded. Take some people who go around for sixty years denying that they have an ego. What a joke! All the time they pay their bills, go about doing their business in the world, and accompanying that is always this notion that the ego doesn't exist. No wonder we have so many schizophrenics!

FD: Instead of denying the I-thought, PB seems to be expanding it.

ANTHONY: Well, he relates it back to its source, relates it to the ideas, to the World-Idea, shows you its significance in terms of both, shows you its relative value. He makes the point that "it cannot be destroyed"—unless you commit suicide, and we're not talking about that. But even then, you just come back, and you'll be in more trouble. The basic point here is that it cannot be destroyed. It has to be enslaved or mastered sooner or later. So you know what your task is, you don't go around trying the ridiculous.

IT IS BOTH true and untrue that we cannot take up the ego with us into the life of mystical illumination. The ego is after all only a reflection, extremely limited and often distorted, of the Higher Self . . . but still it *is* a reflection. If we could bring it into correct alignment with, and submission to, the Higher Self, it would then be no hindrance to the illumined life. The ego cannot, indeed, be destroyed so long as we need its services while in the flesh; but it can be subjugated and turned into a servant instead of permitting it to remain a master. When this is understood, the philosophical ideal of a fully developed, mastered, and richly rounded ego acting as a channel for the inspiration and guidance of the Higher Self will be better appreciated. A poverty-stricken ego will naturally form a more limited channel for the expression of the Higher Self than would a more evolved one. The real enemy to be overcome is not the entity ego, but the function of egoism.

(v6, 8:1.206 AND *Perspectives*, P. 100)

AH: He calls the ego "entity" and he calls egoism "function." Could you amplify that please?

ANTHONY: By entity, he doesn't mean an inherent self-existent. He's simply postulating a matrix of possibilities that can go on evolving.

AH: But for that entity to function, in the body or in the world, as is necessary for even a sage, how is that function not egoism?

ANTHONY: Can you tell the difference between saying this tea is good and I like this tea? Doesn't that exist in us—the ability to impersonally know something, and the same thing known in an egotistical way? The important thing here is that the ego has to be developed, rounded out, filled up with experiences, reach maturation. After all, if you're going to renounce it you want something good so you can say, "Here! This is yours!" You don't want to give the Divine some crumbs. Give a good big solid fat ego. [*laughter*]

The important thing here is to notice that the development of the ego is one thing, egoism is another.

AH: I'm not really clear on that distinction.

ANTHONY: Maybe the direct answer to your question is something like this: the sage has a distinct personality, an ego which you can distinguish from other egos. But then if I ask you, "Is he egoistic?" how would you answer it?

AH: No. I think it is possible for the ego to function without egoism. And that's a hard distinction.

ANTHONY: But we have to see the difference between them. So, for example, someone will come over and say, "Do you like Tchaikovsky's Fifth?" Well I liked it ten years ago, but I hate it now. So I say, "No, that's horrible." That's egoism. The music may be the most appropriate thing in the world for that person at that time, when all I'm expressing is my reactions to my situation.

The ego function of, let's say, listening to the music and appreciating it, absorbing and assimilating it, growing—that's the ego. It has to go through that process. But then the judgements, condemnations, or all the others are unnecessary. That's egoism. This tea is the best because I like it. That's egoism. There's a difference. Fundamentally it comes back to asserting the separateness that you believe yourself to be.

> THERE IS no real ego but only a quick succession of thoughts which constitutes the "I" process. There is no separate entity forming the personal consciousness but only a series of impressions, ideas, images revolving round a common centre. . . .

ANTHONY: So this is your "I"— concepts actualizing themselves from instant to instant. This is what you call your ego.

> . . . The latter is completely empty; the feeling of something being there derives from a totally different plane—that of the Overself.   (v6, 8:2.31)

ANTHONY: What is that empty center he's talking about?

AH: The I-thought.

ANTHONY: But he said the thoughts revolve around it and he referred to it as empty? What is he saying here, what's the center?

FDS: Ultimately it's the Overself.

VM: No, it's a mechanical swirling of thoughts lit up by the Overself.

FDS: It's a misappropriation.

ANTHONY: When you look, when you introspect into yourself, don't you see that there is a nothingness in you? Or do you keep skirting around it? Just look into yourself, just stop for a moment. Haven't you noticed that it's always there, the emptiness that you're running away from?

You're home, you're going to sit down and read a book, you jump up and you run to the bar. What did you run away from? Or you're going to sit down and meditate and you jump up and run out—what did you run away from? What is that emptiness in you? It is certainly not the ego; you wouldn't run away from the ego, you'd run towards it.

AH: Could you say it's in some sense the basis of the ego? The truth or essence of the ego?

ANTHONY: Yes, but that's not relevant here because I'm asking you to identify the point he's making right now. If you haven't noticed this big gaping hole in you, that's not going to help. Not even that sentence is going to help. Hole is a good word. A big black hole in you, did you ever notice it? Or don't you even look that way? What is that center?

FDS: It's a nothingness.

ANTHONY: What is that nothingness?

FDS: I would say it's the primordial error.

ANTHONY: It's your own higher self. You always run away from that emptiness, that loneliness. He's saying just take a look inside yourself, what are you running away from?

AS: You.

ANTHONY: From your Self, yes.

AB: If there wasn't anxiety, it really wouldn't be felt to be empty.

ANTHONY: The anxiety is something else. The anxiety has got to do with the ego, and the fact that the ego recognizes the fact of the possibility of its non-existence. Have you never felt yourself as a hollow man?

AH: But is the feeling of something being there an error?

ANTHONY: No, that's not an error. But that comes from somewhere else. When one looks into his own loneliness, he turns away from it and he's preoccupied with a series of concepts that are actualizing themselves as this I-process. And you become more interested in this process of combustion than you are about that center which is absolutely empty.

> THE EGO to which he is so attached turns out on enquiry to be none other than the presence of World-Mind[4] within his own heart. If identification is then shifted by constant practice from one to the other, he has achieved the purpose of life.　　　(v6, 8:1.127)

FD: Would PB equate those two, the empty center from the previous quote and the World-Mind in the heart from this one?

MB: I thought he said that what the ego takes as its own center is empty on that level, but on another plane there is the presence of the Overself in that center—but not at the same level at which the ego takes it to be.

VM: So the ego's sense of being, or its sense of identity, is coming from another plane—the heart center.

HS: There's a feeling of being that's in each individuality— each heart center, whatever the heart might be.

ANTHONY: There's something we could use as an example.

Think of a dream. We have a series of thoughts one after the other, but they all revolve around the unknown center—the person who's having the dream. The entity in the dream has the feeling that he or she has or is real being.

HS: And the dream itself can continue on the basis of the fact that it's being given real being through the person who has the dream.

ANTHONY: Yes. The reality is coming from the person. The congeries of thoughts is what the dream is all about. And they revolve around the reality of the person. But if you look at the congeries of thoughts and you expect to find a real ego there, all you'll find is one thought after the other. In other words, there's a level of higher being which we're equating with the person, and there's a lesser level or a lower level of being and we're saying that's the dream. The person is immanent in the dream. That immanence gives the ego the feeling that it is *some thing*. That's a misconstruction, a misunderstanding.

MB: Are we saying that that center is not a false idea, but is something that's neutral? So the center itself is an idea maybe, but it's not false?

JB: It's important to know whether the hub is neutral or wonderful or the enemy.

ANTHONY: Let's try another analogy. Imagine a cinema film, and light shining through the film. If it's possible, imagine that the contents within the film all now seem to have an "I." Their I's are based on the fusion of the light in the film. It's the same as we said about the dream. The dream represents a congeries of thoughts, impressions, images, and so on. It is only the immanence in the dream of the person having the dream that now makes it possible for a dream ego to arise. The center of the vortex is *not* neutral. The center of the vortex is the presence of the "I AM" in the matrix of possibilities.

JB: Then that's hardly the enemy.

ANTHONY: For most of us it is the enemy. Because in the matrix of possibilities are all these thoughts, each wants to live its own life, each wants to go its own way.

AS: It's the thoughts themselves, appropriating that light as their own, as if they were that light, which is the egoism.

ANTHONY: Those thoughts have only a past existence or a future possibility. They don't exist in the present. The only thing that exists in that subtle *Now* is this light. Always.

Again, we're back to the problem. The presence of this light *in* thought makes thought think that it is a self-existent entity that has a right to its own view.

On one hand, and this is paradoxical, you have the I AM which is present in the matrix of thoughts. And then the matrix of thoughts takes itself to be the I AM, which it clearly is not. Now that will also account for egoism. That will also make a person think, "Look, I'm superior to everyone else." The consequences are inevitable. Once you accept as separative the congeries of thoughts with that light fused into it, each one is going to think itself superior to every other one. And each thought does. Just like each ego thinks itself superior to every other one.

AH: Anthony, in the case of the bare experience of I AM, in another place PB describes that as immediately being associated with the body and with a world-thought.[5] Is that what you're speaking of?

ANTHONY: Yes.

Now, we've said that the center would be equivalent to the intrusion from a higher level of the I AM. And around that I AM will revolve the "I," the lower personality. That revolution or that construction, that constant self-reconstruction, is what he refers to as the ego. And it can provide itself with all the necessary means and all the necessary material to persist in its own identity. Now what is its identity?

We can go to two quotes. Let's start with the one where he speaks about the wave that separates itself.

THE PERSONAL EGO of man forms itself out of the impersonal life of the universe like a wave forming itself out of the ocean. It constricts, confines, restricts, and limits that infinite life to a small finite area. The wave does just the same to the water of the ocean. The ego shuts out so much of the power and intelligence contained in the universal being that it seems to belong to an entirely different and utterly inferior order of existence. The wave, too, since it forms itself only on the surface of the water gives no indication in its tiny stature of the tremendous depth and breadth and volume of water beneath it.

Consider that no wave exists by itself or for itself, that all waves are inescapably parts of the visible ocean. In the same way, no individual life can separate itself from the All-Life but is always a part of it in some way or other. Yet the idea of separateness is held by millions. This idea is an illusion. From it springs their direst troubles. The work of the quest is simply this: to free the ego from its self-imposed limitations, to let the wave of conscious being subside and straighten itself out into the waters whence it came. The little wave is thus reconverted into the infinite Overself.

(v6, 8:1.102)

DB: He's saying that within the infinite life of the universe there is a specific activity which is limiting that life at a very particular point.

ANTHONY: Yes. There's an infinite life and something is separating itself off from that.

RG: What ontological status does this separative power of the wave *per se* have?

AB: The ego is based on a real principle which we're saying is the Overself.

ANTHONY: Yes, but is *egoism* based on a real principle?

HS: The question is: What gives the wave its power to take itself as other—which it intrinsically is not?

ANTHONY: If we say that the ocean gives rise to waves, and is their support, is their ground, then the next point is that something occurs here: This life differentiated out of this cosmic life now can speak of itself as separate from the rest. Now isn't that the point?

RG: Yes.

ANTHONY: And is that the problem? So then it's the attachment, the emotional attachment, to this separation that it itself conceives? That around this revolves egoism?

If you think of life as an infinite ocean that gives rise to waves, the waves are not separated from the ocean—they're part of the ocean. But that a wave should conceive of itself as distinct from the ocean and other than the ocean—that's where you would have to look for the problem. The problem certainly doesn't exist in the ocean. So this arisal of the feeling of separateness from the ocean is something going on within that wave. There's no hiatus between the wave and the ocean even though the wave thinks there is. And this thinking keeps going on.

The point here is that it's the emotional attachment to this separativeness that is the problem.

MB: Is it a metaphysical or emotional problem?

ANTHONY: You have to tell me what you mean by emotional, because that's the whole point we're getting at. The ego is dependent on that emotional attachment to its separateness. That's what keeps it going. Otherwise if a person could understand that metaphysically—he should be released. Right? But it doesn't work like that. The emotional attachment persists. If that emotional support was taken away, you would feel like you were falling into an abyss.

VM: And isn't that emotional support connected to the body?

ANTHONY: It can be, but not necessarily. Everything that's done by the ego will lend support to that attachment, that emotional attachment to the separative tendencies. That's the hard one. That's tracing it back to its lair.

AH: Do we feel ourself to be separate because we have our own Overself, or because we have our own ego?

HS: Do you think the felt separateness belongs to the Overself?

AH: I think that the perpetuity—the necessity for continuity—has its origin in the Overself.

HS: You're saying it's the Overself that likes it down here?

ANTHONY: No. I think what we could say is that if the soul is bliss and peace and if the ego is these thought tendencies that envelop and wrap themselves around this bliss, then that ego would take itself to be a separative entity in its own right and that's a case of misplaced feeling, or ignorance.

HS: So the ego appropriates the feeling of bliss to itself?

ANTHONY: Yes. Is that so? Or isn't it? Do we or don't we worship our ego?

AH: But it's not experienced as bliss! [*laughter*]

ANTHONY: You don't experience it as bliss? I dare you to say that out loud again. You don't worship the ego, right?

AH: Oh, yes. But frequently, Anthony, it's not a very pleasant experience.

ANTHONY: That could be, yes, but does that stop you? You value the ego so much.

RG: Don't you love the suffering?

ANTHONY: Even your suffering won't separate you from it. [*pause*] Well, I think now it would be appropriate to read the next quote.

THE EGO is after all only an idea. It derives its seeming
actuality from a higher source. If we make the inner
effort to search for its origin we shall eventually find the

Mind in which this idea originated. That mind is the
Overself. This search is the Quest. The self-separation
of the idea from the mind which makes its existence
possible, is egoism.   (v6, 8:1.9)

HS: Would you equate mind and infinite life in this way?

ANTHONY: You mean mind and soul. Yes, you could use
the term mind as soul here.

AH: Is it being said that the separation between Overself
and ego is equal to the separation between mind and idea?

ANTHONY: Yes.

RG: But wouldn't you have to call it egoism only when the
idea takes itself not to be grounded in mind?

ANTHONY: Yes.

AS: It's just a bundle of thoughts, but what imparts to
the bundle of thoughts its feeling of having a real continuing
existence, of an "I," is that Overself. And then that bundle of
thoughts takes itself to be that which gives itself that feeling.

ANTHONY: Once it takes itself to be that bundle of
thoughts, it cuts itself off from the ocean.

AH: How could that idea take itself to be anything else
than what it is? And how can it correct itself?

ANTHONY: Self-will. To your first question, self-will. Go
over what you said: What is there *in* it that makes it take itself
to be *other* than it *is*? You've got to look it straight in the eyes.

JC: Is that principle of separation inherent . . .

ANTHONY: *It's not a principle!*

JC: Isn't the self-will you're speaking of inherent in the soul
itself? The tendency to break away from contemplation, to
look toward the lower worlds?

ANTHONY: I don't want to get into metaphysics. I want to
keep it at this level of egoism. Yes, every soul has its own desires, and accedes to them, and descends into manifestation,
and I don't want to get into that. Deviate and you'll lose it.

You'll get caught up in all the subtle urges that the ego wants to practice.

The question was asked: How can the idea take itself to be other than it is? And I said, that's the answer. That's the ego.

JB: I'd like to understand how the answer is the question itself. If you could focus on the mechanism that generates this sense of separateness, then that is a likely resource for the remedy. I wonder if getting rid of the emotional attachment is enough?

ANTHONY: Yes. But the revelation that you can even recognize the mechanism that is being used, will eventually focus your attention on the fact that it's an emotional attachment that separates you from everything else. But that is going to be very difficult to perceive. You're not going to see that. You only have that experience when you go through what they call the mystical death. The second mystical death, when the ego dies thoroughly, is the entrance into the void. There the emotional attachment is cut off.

I think the point you're making is very worthwhile—to recognize the mechanism. Because it's one of the clear signals. It's like a bell—you get to know that mechanism and you can always see that the ego's active behind that mechanism because it becomes stereotyped. But once you recognize *that*, it will use another mechanism. You're not going to get to it easily.

A lot of people think that all they need to do is take out their sword and cut off its head. You can use an A-bomb and you won't succeed.

IF WE HAVE WRITTEN of the ego as if it were a separate
and special entity, a fixed thing, a reality in its own
right, this is only because of the inescapable necessities
of logical human thinking and the inexorable limitations of traditional human language. For in FACT the
"I" cannot be separated from its thoughts since it is

composed of them, and them alone. The ego is, in
short, only an idea, or a trick that the thought process
plays on itself.   (v6, 8:2.46 AND *Perspectives*, P. 101)

ANTHONY: How do you like that? It's a trick that the ego
plays on itself.

HS: I don't like that at all.

ANTHONY: I don't blame you.

AB: Within the thought process that produces the ego, the
ego seems to be more than a thought. It seems to be the holder
of the thought or the producer of the thought. Wouldn't that
be the sense in which it was a trick played on itself?

ANTHONY: It's a thought that believes in itself.

HS: So Alan [AB], you would say that your ego is inside the
continuum, the mental stream, and appropriates parts of it.

ANTHONY: It *is* the continuum, not inside the continuum.
Within the functioning of a matrix of those possibilities, one
of them is that it's going to believe in its own validity. You've
seen that in many psychotics, right—"I'm Napoleon!"

HS: And it's an objective process? Like the way a circle
might inhere in an object?

AB: The ego is a thought just like all the other thoughts
but in my everyday experience the ego seems to be the subject which has the thoughts, and the thoughts appear to belong
to or relate to the ego. That is the sense in which it's a trick.

ANTHONY: If the ego is a bunch of thoughts that are constantly externalizing themselves, then one of the things that
they have a belief in is its own reality. That's what's going on
all the time. The ego's a bunch of thoughts constantly externalizing and manifesting themselves and corporealizing
themselves and believing in itself. What's wrong? Isn't that a
perfect description of our behavior?

HS: I think the whole thing is wrong. But the description
is quite accurate.

ANTHONY: It's accurate, yes.

HS: I think the interesting thing is that a thought could actually appropriate, attach, keep you in bondage. This is an interesting kind of thought.

ANTHONY: That's why it has to be taken seriously. It's like a snake pit.

DB: It doesn't seem like the ego is one thought amongst all the others.

ANTHONY: That's why I call it a matrix of possibilities actualizing themselves continuously and uninterruptedly and believing in that actualization. You could almost say that in the very instant where you have a subject-object relationship—a thought which would include both—the whole of the matrix of possibilities, or this nucleated structure of thought, is present in that one instant and the next instant and the next instant. And so it goes on perpetuating its belief in itself, which, when we inquire into it, is enough to frighten us all.

> WHEN it is declared that the ego is a fictitious entity,
> what is meant is that it does not exist as a real entity.
> Nevertheless, it does exist as a thought.   (v6, 8:2.32)

AH: So from that perspective, if the ego is at base this thought, how can part of the ego disassociate itself from another part of itself?

ANTHONY: You're doing what he tells you not to do. He tells you the ego is not a permanent entity. So now you say it's a thought and you make that a permanent entity.

AH: From the point of view of living a better life, how shall I jump over my own shoulders?

ANTHONY: Don't you do that when you meditate? You use one thought to try to put down the other thoughts. So you say a *japa*, you say a mantram, *Om Bitsu*. That's a thought. And the purpose of that thought is to stop and block all the other thoughts, to reduce the multiplicity of thoughts to one thought. So if you keep saying *Om Bitsu* intensely enough and with enough perseverance, that thought becomes dominant. All the other thoughts subside in comparison to that. Now you have only one thought to work with, whereas before you had millions.

AH: Anthony, if you're successful in that exercise and reduce it to one thought, is that one thought still the root of the ego?

ANTHONY: No. Let me ask you something. Someone praises me or criticizes me. Let's say they criticize me, and at that moment I feel hurt. That feeling of being hurt, that's the ego. If you want to grab it with your fingers, go ahead and try. But the next instant, the same person will say what a nice guy I am. Now I feel good. There's the ego again. Are you going to grab that with your two hands and embrace it? You keep trying to make a thing out of this. In both cases, it just slipped by. It's necessary to understand its elusive nature.

Remember the Zen story of the man who came over to the teacher and told him he was egoless, and the teacher started pouring the tea? He filled up the cup and it started overflowing and the man was getting mad. It was the ego. And the teacher did that very deliberately. "Oh, you have no ego?" And he kept pouring the tea out. [*laughter*] But if you try to grasp it, where is it? This conflict is ever present in all thoughts or in any number of them, and the conflict could always go on. But don't look for some *thing*. You won't find it. Try to remember, though, the basic thing is that in meditation you do this all the time. You use one thought to subdue all the other thoughts.

AH: The example of meditation can be understood. But how can we subjugate thought or ego when we're not meditating?

ANTHONY: You can try to take a witness position. This is the secret doctrine. The others are quite exoteric.

AH: When you describe the ego as part of the World-Idea, there's a way of describing the whole scenario and there shouldn't be any problem whatsoever. But there's an enormous problem that we each experience on a personal level, the problem of wanting to understand and all that. What is it that's specifically wrong? We talk about attachment to the ego. What's attached to it?

ANTHONY: It's attached to itself.

NG: It likes itself.

ANTHONY: No, you're wrong. It doesn't like itself, it *loves* itself, it worships itself, it adores itself. What's wrong? Well, with that kind of attitude you're never going to have a cosmic or an impersonal point of view. Obviously.

AH: With what kind of attitude?

ANTHONY: With the attitude of self-adoration.

Each and every one of us is going to have to see for ourself what the ego is. Of course, if you keep looking for some *thing* I don't think you're going to find it. But take the example I just gave when I spoke about how someone praises you and you feel good—in that feeling good, you can *smell* its presence right there. Because in the next instance someone is going to criticize you and you'll feel bad and you'll ask yourself, "Why do I feel bad?" Well, who is it that feels bad? And every time these feelings come around, you'll get to know them little by little.

You know, you meet a nice pretty girl, and you take her to the cafeteria and have coffee and you're feeling good. Who's that feeling good? You know. You'll get to know him. If you look at it right then and there instead of being preoccupied with feeling good or feeling bad, you might be able to see how elusive it is.

AH: You say that feeling good, bad, or indifferent doesn't have any foundation in anything except himself.

ANTHONY: That's the whole point. The foundation is in

himself, in his ego. I feel good! I just had this nice warm cup of coffee. Who's that creature, crawling around, sliding, insinuating itself, every remark, every thought, every glance, every memory? Who is it? Are you asking me, "Show it to me?" I can't, go look for yourself. Maybe a mirror might help.

Someone says something to you, you get angry and ask yourself: Who is it that got angry? See if you can come up with somebody. You'll see that no sooner do you know it was there, the next instant it isn't. Because the next thought is another thought. The vitality of that thought, we sometimes call the dragon, and he's very crafty and sly. He just goes from one thought to another, makes himself at home in all of them. And he has many disguises, many hiding places.

That's why I call this the secret doctrine. And it's the most crucial part of the teaching. Because the difference between being on the right-hand path and the left-hand path is to know the difference between these two.

AH: Which are these two?

ANTHONY: The ego.

AH: And?

ANTHONY: Whether you're serving yourself or the Higher.

You understand that the ego is *the* problem. You know that, don't you? Unless you understand this, you're going *nowhere!* You can go to all the pilgrimages you want, you can see all the sages you want, you can do *anything* you want. But unless you deal with this, you're not getting or going anywhere.

ALTHOUGH THE EGO claims to be engaged in a war against itself, we may be certain that it has no intention of allowing a real victory to be achieved but only a pseudo-victory. The simple conscious mind is no match for such cunning. This is one reason why out of so many spiritual seekers, so few really attain union with

the Overself, why self-deceived masters soon get a
following whereas the true ones are left in peace,
untroubled by such eagerness.

(v6, 8:4.316 AND *Perspectives*, P. 98)

ANTHONY: THE SIMPLE MIND IS NO MATCH FOR
THE CUNNING OF THE EGO. You could write that and
put it alongside your bed. When you get up in the morning,
look at that first. Because you're going to lose—by the end of
the night you'll lose.

The conscious mind that you're operating with now is no
match for your ego, which has the resources of all prior perception and experience. If the conscious mind that you're
working with now posits itself against the ego, it will be defeated on the simple grounds that the ego's experiences are
vast, vast in comparison to the experiences that your conscious mind has.

DB: I'm, you know, thirty, or whatever.

ANTHONY: And the ego's about two million years old.

If you think in a historical way, think of the vast eons of
time in which this evolving entity has learned to survive re-
gardless of what the conditions were. Now this evolving entity,
through periods of time that are unimaginable, has learned to
survive through any and every condition.

Think what it has at its disposal. It will outwit you any
time, any day, any place, anywhere. It has learned every possible trick of how to survive, even into the twenty-first
century. As soon as it is threatened in any way, it already
has this vast reservoir of how it's outwitted previous circumstances, situations, events, animals, people—whatever—all at
its disposal to use against you.

LR: But PB calls this a "fictitious" entity?

ANTHONY: Well, by that he means it has no real permanence, because we can think of it as a life that is continuously

flowing and that isn't any static entity—if you think of it in that way. But the gist that you'll get as you read through these notes on the ego is: If you say it's "illusory," you're going to put big quotation marks around the word.

AH: Isn't that what's meant by its "survival"—that it prevents perception of it as illusory?

ANTHONY: Yes, of course.

AH: So it has to be real good at what it does in order to continue.

ANTHONY: I'm quite sure we're acquainted with that. That's why I sometimes tease you by saying that anyone who tells me the ego is illusory is out of his mind. He hasn't even encountered it yet.

BS: But that encounter is required for the revulsion to take place.

ANTHONY: What becomes repulsive about it is its nature, how it can completely disregard the consequences of any activity it might engage in, whether to its owner or to anyone else. Remember the other quote where he says that it "lies to itself, lies to the man who identifies himself with it, and lies to other men." [v6, 8:3.83 and *Perspectives*, p. 100] Little by little, as you begin to pick up pieces of what the ego is like, you're not going to be exactly enamored of it.

DB: I don't understand how the ego gets so cunning.

ANTHONY: If you say that the ego is the sum total of the tendencies left behind from previous existences, and you start from the time that you were an amoeba and work your way up through the tree of life, by this time you would have acquired every trick in the book. "Cunning" is a British understatement.

DD: On one hand we talk about the ego as a matrix of thought. On the other hand, it acts. Where does its dynamism come from?

ANTHONY: It's inherent when you say tendency. Otherwise you're thinking of tendency as a very static concept.

If I could employ the example of a rolled-up paper that I put under the bed: When I take it out and stretch it, it rolls up again. Very dynamic. It keeps fighting all the way. Don't think of thought, don't think of the residue of past existences as incapable of that profound dynamism. It's so profound that we can hardly withstand it. I mean, we accept it as absolutely natural to our being. Just like your eyelids close and things like that. In biology they use the term "tropism." The other term would be "irritability of protoplasm." [*laughter*]

AH: Its activity, its dynamism, is part of its own built-in defense mechanism.

ANTHONY: It's fundamental to the matrix. Even the sage loves his existence. He may not want to continue it one moment after he's supposed to not continue it, but up to that moment he loves his existence, just like an ant, or an amoeba—fundamental facts of life.

> JUNG thought he had found, in what he called the
> unconscious, the source which twisted, negated, or
> opposed the ego's ideals. This source was the shadow.
> He needed to go farther and deeper for then he would
> have known the shadow to be the ego itself. (v6, 8:3.29)

ANTHONY: We saw the same thing, if you remember. Very often I refer to the ego as the same as the shadow. The ego is the shadow projected by the light of the soul coming through the personality. And if you want to make this distinction within it, you're welcome to do so. You'll have to remember that they're aspects of one and the same thing.

> THE EGO is by nature a deceiver and in its operations a
> liar. For if it revealed things as they really are, or told
> what is profoundly true, it would have to expose its own

self as the arch-trickster pretending to be the man
himself and proffering the illusion of happiness.

(v6, 8:3.79 AND *Perspectives*, P. 106)

ANTHONY: I made a remark some time ago that the only
time I consider a person a quester is when he recognizes the
ego. Until he knows who his enemy is, he's just imagining
he's a quester. But once he knows who his enemy is, then the
decision will come: Am I going to fight this or join it? Not
before. I'm talking about something that's happening right
now, in these classes, the confrontation with what we are. You
like it? Sign up. You don't like it? Sign up. One way or another
you're going to have to draw a line now. What side do you
want to be on? You're going to make a choice one way or
another.

CS: Couldn't it be that the ego sets up these traps that
cause us pain so that we eventually will look inward?

ANTHONY: No. The ego will never accept the consequences of what it does. It's a real delusion to think that the
ego is going to try to encourage you to inquire into its nature.
Because it will immediately present you with another desire.
And then when you get hurt with that one it will give you
another one. That devaluation is going to be really very momentary. You get hurt, and after an hour you're right back in
it all over again. You say, "Wow, the world really isn't such a
hot place," but within an hour, you're right back. Even for
those people who have a tremendous loss and devalue the
world, it's momentary. Two days later, three days later, the
ego is right back there. The world has got all the glamour all
over again. Don't tell me that this ego is going to present you
with a desire which if you fulfill it will hurt you and then
cause you to turn inward. PB didn't say the ego was the
Overself. It's a mishap, it's a bad reflection.

SA: So who is it that pursues meditation or imposes
discipline?

ANTHONY: You, YOU! Your ego, *you.*

FS: So the ego is going to deceive itself and annihilate itself?

ANTHONY: It's not deceiving itself. It's going to make out. It's going to accommodate you. "Oh, we'll sit down, we'll meditate." After a while, you're fast asleep.

But let's say you don't fall asleep. Let's say you have a magnificent experience, all right? It's *your* experience, right? The ego appropriated it completely. No longer is it an experience or something given to you, "It's MY experience."

DR: But the ego is also doing the exercise.

ANTHONY: In other words, when you're carrying on some practical exercise, like the remembrance exercise, that's the ego. Yes, sure, and PB has a quote, for instance, where he points out that the ego will even submit to this abasement, providing it can continue living![6]

DR: That brings in a difficulty, because there you're trying to distinguish one class of thoughts from another.

ANTHONY: What's difficult about that? What do you think the ego is, one thought? I call it a matrix of possibilities so that we avoid turning it into a *thing*. It has many facets, many aspects.

How many I's do you have? You ever notice yourself? "I want this"; ten minutes later, "I want that"; and ten minutes later, "I want the other thing." Now which "I" wants what? And which "I" is "I"?

If you keep falling back, thinking of the ego as a thing, you're going to get into all these kinds of difficulties. But if you think of it the way we spoke about it—as a bunch of tendencies insisting upon their survival, and working towards it all the time—and if you reach a point where you say, "Darn it, you're not going to get any further with me," the ego says, "OK, I'll submit; you want to meditate, let's meditate." Then when you really get into meditation and you get carried and you're really going well, the ego comes right over and says, "Well, I think this fellow has taken me far enough."

DR: In every possible human experience there's a reflex of thoughts that will appropriate it.

ANTHONY: So it's always going on, all the way up. The ego is accommodating itself to these tendencies so that it doesn't get removed. It will do anything as long as it can continue. You've heard of the instinct of self-preservation, "I above all else"? So what's wrong with the ego saying, "All right, I'll accommodate myself to this higher trance state; you know, what am I going to do with this guy?" [*laughter*] So then you go into this high trance state and you come out and you think you are the new messiah! Now, who's there? Of course!

I never said it was a nice clean fight with every blow above the belt. Every step along the way you go up, the ego goes up with you. And at each level you're going to have a struggle with it. Sometimes it'll take you down a peg or two, or maybe three or four.

RG: But on one hand you say, I'm going to sit this ego down and it's going to meditate with me.

ANTHONY: No, you don't say that. You say, "I." "I, this ego is going to sit down and meditate." Certain tendencies within you are beginning to show their manifestation. You desire to meditate. That's part of the matrix of tendencies that you have. Why? Because maybe you suffered enough and decided somewhere in the dim past that you want to figure a way out. Maybe you didn't suffer enough. Maybe you saw some beauty that you could never see on earth and you decided that's what you want. I don't know why, but I do know that all of a sudden you say, "I want to sit down and meditate." So you sit down and meditate.

WITH ONE PART of himself he honestly seeks truth, but with another part he tries to evade it.   (v6, 8:4.106)

FRD: Is this passage saying that the one part of him that

seeks truth is not coming from the ego? It has to come through the ego, it has to be manifested through this field, but is its source not the ego?

ANTHONY: No, he's saying that it's coming from the ego. There's a part of you that wants the truth, there are other parts that don't. We spoke about that as generating a continuum within the ego of a certain stream of thought. And if you persist, this insistence to want to find the truth becomes a residue or part of your personality. It will be with and among other tendencies, but it's part of the ego. It's the ego that wants to know the truth.

BEING WHAT it is, a compound of higher and lower attributes which are perpetually in conflict, the ego has no assured future other than that of total collapse. The Bible sentence, "A Kingdom divided against itself cannot stand," is very applicable to it: this is why the aspirant must take heart that one day his goal will be reached, even if there were no law of evolution to confirm it— as there is. (v6, 8:4.397)

ANTHONY: There's a kind of internal neurosis in the ego. We're never quite integrated. There are always different parts. This part of the ego wants this and another part of the ego wants that. If we think of the ego as tendencies, a matrix of tendencies, there would be tendencies that want the truth and there would be tendencies that want a new pair of wings. There would be tendencies that want money, that want material things. And it's a hotbed of all these tendencies. You have to decide which ones to reinforce.

THE EGO's sphere of activity is fivefold—thought, imagination, memory, feeling, and action. (v6, 8:3.5)

ANTHONY: We want to try to get a look at the way it works, what characterizes it, what its attributes are. You can keep cutting down one desire after another, but if you don't get to the root it just keeps spreading more branches.

THE PERSONA, the mask which he presents to the world, is only one part of his ego. The conscious nature, composed of thoughts and feelings, is the second part. The hidden store of tendencies, impulses, memories, and ideas—formerly expressed and then reburied, or brought over from earlier lives, and all latent—is the third part.　　　　(v6, 8:3.17 AND *Perspectives*, P. 102)

ANTHONY: The psychosomatic organism plus the traces of memory—that's a way of understanding the ego.

THE PERSONALITY is rooted in the Overself. Hence its own power and movement do reflect, albeit minutely, slightly, and distortedly, some of the Overself's own attributes.　　　　(v6, 8:1.139)

AH: But there are just as many quotes that take another view. Rather than espousing this holistic view of the ego, they suggest that it has to be seen as unreal before the philosophic work can begin.

ANTHONY: But that's the point I'm making. He's working on the notion of the ego from all sides. Think of that as the center of the circle, and the circumference has the various perspectives that one may and should have about the ego. It should be a view of the 360 degrees: from all sides, beneath, below, above, from every possible perspective and angle—instead of what we referred to as the clichés and the propaganda and all these ridiculous things that tell you nothing about what the ego is, what it's up to, where it's going, and what it wants to do.

CHAPTER ONE \ 41

AH: But if the task is to establish a perspective, and in doing that we agree that the ego is both real and unreal . . .

ANTHONY: He didn't say it's real and unreal. He said what it is: It's a thought, and as a thought it exists and as an existence it must be dealt with. Then he goes ahead and says: But it's not a real thing, it's not a permanent entity. Those are the exigencies of language, which force us to think that it's a thing. Both sides of the argument are covered, whether it is real or whether it isn't real. And he tells you what it is: a thought. Saying it's unreal will make you think it doesn't exist, and he doesn't want you to think that. So the whole approach that he uses and the language that he uses put you on the track. He doesn't get you into what we call *grooves* of thinking.

AH: Would it be correct, then, to summarize and say it does exist but it's not real?

ANTHONY: Yes.

> THE ROOT of all the trouble is not man's wickedness or animality or cunning greedy mind. It is his very I-ness, for all those other evils grow out of it. It is his own ego. Here is the extraordinary and baffling self-contradiction of the human situation. It is man's individual existence which brings him suffering and yet it is this very existence which he holds as dear as life to him!
>
> (V7, 11:2.22 AND *Perspectives*, P. 139)

ANTHONY: Just keep repeating that. That's the mystery exposed, isn't it? Could you reread it, a little at a time?

> The root of all the trouble is not man's wickedness or animality or cunning greedy mind. It is his very I-ness . . .

ANTHONY: "I-ness." But "I-ness" here is used in the sense of ego. For PB, the way you get to truth is by penetrating into the nature of a paradox. So let's try. "His very I-ness." Now

that I-ness we're trying to understand—in the next sentence
he says it is his ego?

> . . . for all those other evils grow out of it. It is his own
> ego . . .

ANTHONY: Now, what would this ego be then? We know
it's a collection of thoughts, right? But a collection of thoughts
standing by themselves would be meaningless. I mean, it just
doesn't make any sense to say a collection of thoughts is an
ego. There has to be some consciousness permeating or per-
vading those thoughts in order to speak about an ego, an I-
ness. But if you remove the consciousness or the mind which
pervades those thoughts, then you would have no ego. I
mean, if I was able to subtract the consciousness that permeates you, then all I would have there would be a ghost, a skel-
eton, a collection of a lot of thoughts—all right? You've got
no ego. So this ego seems to be a mixture of two things: a collection of thoughts on one hand, and a fixed and empty center
[consciousness] on the other.

So let's continue. Let's see if we see the nature of this
paradox. You see, you're going to be a mixture of good and
bad. In your case more bad than good! [*laughter*]

> . . . Here is the extraordinary and baffling self-
> contradiction of the human situation . . .

ANTHONY: Notice the terms he's using? "*Extraordinary*,"
"*baffling*." You could even say impossible. How could such a
thing as a divine reality and this cluster of thoughts come
together to make this ego? It's a paradox.

> . . . It is man's individual existence . . .

ANTHONY: Stop there. "*It is man's individual existence.*" In other words, when the soul of a man identifies with some particle of the World-Idea, then it takes on an individual existence . . .

AS: Or it seems to.

ANTHONY: Or it seems to. That's good enough, "It seems to."

AS: Or, "*It takes on.*"

ANTHONY: They're very close. It seems to take on this individual existence when, say, this reality identifies with this cluster of thoughts, all right? So, on one hand, you have the soul which can be in itself and, on the other hand, you have the soul as identified with this cluster of thoughts which is part of the World-Idea which is evolving. Maybe it's not evolving. I just want to carry on a rear guard. Go ahead.

TS: The consciousness that pervades those thoughts . . .

ANTHONY: That wouldn't be the ego. That consciousness would be the divinity. Now you've got two things, like a mixture. On one hand you have the soul, and on the other hand you have that which belongs to the World-Idea, a cluster of thoughts. These two are mixed together, and you have an individual existence.

TS: The individuality of that existence is provided only by the thoughts?

ANTHONY: It's provided by the mixture. Once you have the mixture, then you have the individuality. If the consciousness does not associate or permeate or identify with a cluster of thoughts, you don't have an individual.

I use the word "permeation," although "identification" could be used. But when we think of this mind or soul as permeating, or think of this light which is illuminating everything in a room yet has no relationship with any of the objects in the room . . . in a similar way, the mind is permeating all these thoughts that we call our ego-structure. But there's no real relationship. It isn't that you can relate A through B to C, because this is not a thing.

RG: There are distinctions within the soul that allow for the varying degrees of identification.

ANTHONY: Well, that would depend on the level of the soul's evolution. One soul would identify with these thoughts immediately. Another soul would do so hesitantly. Another one would oppose it.

RG: It doesn't all come from the side of the World-Idea.

ANTHONY: Here again, we could think of it as a mixture. We could think of it coming mutually. We could think of the thoughts, or the tendencies, which we spoke about as a kind of matter that foists itself on the soul or the mind. There has to be an inherent tendency in it to do so, just like there would be an inherent tendency within the soul to identify with those tendencies. So again you'd have a mutual mixture of the soul identifying with a cluster of tendencies and the tendencies having a proclivity to claim consciousness for its own. So there you have this mixture which produces an individual. And this is the strange part: Now it is this individual, this combination of two things, which is going to be the source of our suffering, the source of our learning, the source of our evolution. It's a paradox. It's the reality that you are, involved in those tendencies.

> . . . It is man's individual existence which brings him
> suffering and yet it is this very existence which he holds
> as dear as life to him!

ANTHONY: What do you say you love more than anything else?

TS: Myself. My own existence.

ANTHONY: Your own ego? That is the very thing that is the cause of all the suffering we would go through, and yet we love it more than anything else, and we would not part from it—not willingly. Isn't that paradoxical? I know of nothing that gives more pain than the ego, and I know of nothing that I love more than that ego.

JA: You said that the ego wraps itself around a portion of infinite bliss and calls it its own and somehow pain results from that. If it's so painful, why is it held so dear?

ANTHONY: He's talking about the paradoxical situation we find ourselves in. We love that which gives us more pain than anything else!

NH: The pain is because we are separated from the Overself.

ANTHONY: Honestly, do you experience pain because you're separated from the Overself, especially if you never knew it? We don't know the Overself, so let's not talk about the pain of the separation from the Overself. We *do* know the pain that's delivered daily, hourly, weekly, monthly, and yearly. We do know that pain, and that comes from our own ego. And this is what we love, despite the fact that it's delivering the punches all the time. Is this or is it not a paradox?

NH: It's a paradox.

ANTHONY: And that's what we are, a paradox.

JB: If what we love is a source of pain, isn't there something to learn in that?

ANTHONY: But now you're speaking like an optimist. The fact is, we don't stop loving it. No matter how much pain we suffer from it, we go on loving it even more intensely. Go ahead, I know you're going to be an optimist; you're going to bring in Grace. I'm trying to make it miserable for everybody. [*laughter*]

It's fundamental that you understand PB's notes on the ego. I don't care who else you read, they just don't talk about this item. As a matter of fact, one person who should have known better said, "You don't want to deliver this kind

of stuff. You don't want to see it published—it's too harsh."
Sure, let's publish some more comic strips.

MB: Do we really know that it's the ego that's giving us that pain?

ANTHONY: Well, I assume that you recognize what the ego is first. The ordinary person will not understand that; he won't consider that a paradox. But you're not ordinary. Go ahead, [to student who wanted to talk about Grace] they need encouragement. [*laughter*]

AP: Isn't the pain we feel because we know inwardly there's something divine in us? Isn't that true?

KD: I don't think so. I suffer because I don't get what I want, or my job is bad, or my husband is bad, or I blame it on my kids or circumstances. I think it's a real dirty deal, in a way.

ANTHONY: Well, that's because you haven't recognized the value of suffering yet. Then you might not feel it's such a dirty deal.

KD: You mean we should all enjoy our suffering?

ANTHONY: I think you missed the point. You said you didn't get what you want, and that makes you unhappy. The point is: You *want*; that's what makes you unhappy. You experience joy the moment your wish is gratified, because you let go of desire.

KD: But you're forced to want, you're put into this body.

ANTHONY: No, nobody has to be here if they don't want to. *No one* has to be here unless they want to be here. You *want* to be here. [*chuckling*] No, you're here because you love your ego. The suffering is a concomitant.

BS: By "here" you mean ego-centered.

ANTHONY: I mean here. HERE. I don't care if you point to your body, point to this room, point to your house, point to the planet: You're *here*.

KD: God help us all!

ANTHONY: He tries very hard. [*pause*]

See, the theory here is quite different than, for instance, the Christian version. You know, the version that the creation of an entity, the soul and the body, is a fiat on the part of God . . . that when He creates a soul the body comes with it and the two of them are conjoined and it's an eternal union. Nothing like this is involved here. This is a whole different concept. And it's really quite a paradox. That's why it's so beautiful. It remains a mystery, no matter how you try to get out of it. Even the sage suffers.

NOTES

1. The divine soul in the human being.

2. Paul Brunton, whose notes on the ego form the basis of discussion in these classes.

3. The deepest, thought-free, state of contemplation.

4. PB's term for God as manifesting and manifested by the entire universe.

5. See *The Wisdom of the Overself,* Chapter 6, paragraph 13.

6. Reference is to *The Notebooks of Paul Brunton,* volume 6, part 1, Chapter 4, #309. See also same chapter, number 313 and number 167. The latter appears also on pp. 199-200 of the present book.

THE EGO STANDS IN THE WAY: its own presence annuls awareness of the presence of the Overself. But this need not be so. Correct and deeper understanding of what the self is, proper adjustment between the individual and the universal in consciousness, will bring enlightenment.

(v6, 8:4.369)

CHAPTER TWO

OBJECTIFYING
THE EGO

HE MUST START by admitting with complete frankness
that the ego worships not God but itself, and that it
carries this idolatry into a Church, if religious, or onto
the Quest, if mystical.   (v6, 8:3.133)

ANTHONY: If you think you can exaggerate the value of this
bit of information you're crazy. We've *got* to hear it.

The ego carries this idolatry everywhere. Everywhere—
no exceptions. Church, philosophies, psychology, business,
home—anywhere and everywhere. The only place it can't
carry it is in the thought-free state.

CD: Would even any feeling of devotion be the ego?
Anything that could manifest in consciousness is the ego?

ANTHONY: Yes, yes, on and on. All the way up. But that
doesn't take away the value of devotion.

NG: In which sense does it not?

ANTHONY: In the sense that you're trying to get out of
your ego.

RC: Your devotion doesn't have to be glued to some image.

ANTHONY: As a matter of fact, the ideal way to carry on
devotion is not to have any images, and to remain passively
what you are.

CD: I think PB says in *The Wisdom of the Overself* that the only true worship is silence.

ANTHONY: Yes, if you could manage that.

RC: His conception of the divine is not any kind of mental form, not any kind of idea that you can become hypnotized by.

ANTHONY: It's a virginal mind.

RC: Yet the ego demands: "I want a concrete image, a concrete feeling, something very definitive."

ANTHONY: And we know that those are all states of the ego. Even if the ego is very highly evolved, and has beautiful aspirations, it's still within the realm of the ego.

> THE EGO not only obligingly provides him with a
> spiritual path to keep him busy for several years and
> thus keeps him from tracking it down to its lair; it
> even provides him with a spiritual illumination to
> authenticate that path. Need it be said that this counter-
> feit illumination is another form of the ego's own
> aggrandizement?   (v6, 8:4.321 AND *Perspectives*, P. 99)

MB: Is this quote saying that the ego provides the Long Path, or that the ego provides a fake path?

ANTHONY: The ego can do both. It can provide you with a long path, short path, fake path. It will make you think that you are the noblest. It can justify anything.

LR: In mystical experience the ego is still there?

ANTHONY: It will come right in and take over your mystical experiences. That's why it's so dangerous to have mystical experience without metaphysical training. Just go back in your past to all the times you've been "illuminated" by the ego. Think over the things that you did which you thought were spiritual and then were corrected for you.

It'll suddenly tell you: "Look! You're wasting your time studying the doctrine. You should be out exploring the world and making your way to the top of the pyramid, and that's spiritual." It could come in any form. It could come in any way.

CDA: But he's not speaking about the kind of mystical experience that the ego has the power to evoke?

ANTHONY: That, too, could take place. You could have a mystical experience, a true authentic glimpse of the Overself, and it could be completely distorted by what the ego brings to bear on it. As a matter of fact, the ego is there—present, inter-penetrating—and is immediate in its response to what you're seeing. So the reality you experience and your interpretation of it are two different things.

CDA: That's something different than the ego having the power to have . . .

ANTHONY: But isn't that the power? Isn't that POWER? All of a sudden you get a glimpse and you say, "I'm the new messiah." And it creates visions for you. It does it every night!

LR: The quote said the ego could provide a spiritual illumination.

RG: A counterfeit one!

DB: How do you differentiate between true and counterfeit illuminations?

ANTHONY: Did you ever listen to some of these preachers on television? The ego has provided them with a "spiritual" path and also with a "spiritual" illumination. In this matter, there is no spirituality. That's one example. The ego's going to trick you. It doesn't want you to get onto the path, and it's going to provide you with enough thrills and exaltations to make you think that you *are* on it. It's got nothing to do with being on the path.

JNL: What differentiates phony illuminations from real ones?

ANTHONY: Well, qualitatively they're quite different. There is the exaltation that one experiences when his ego's going to provide him with some kind of thrill—"Look at the great work I'm doing: That man dropped his crutches and walked over to me." Then the following week there is no such man, and you pay somebody to drop his crutches and walk over to you. We're talking about that kind of path that the ego can provide. But the differentiation of an authentic experience is a given thing that's outside of the ego. As a matter of fact, the precondition for it is that the ego isn't there.

JNL: Even afterwards?

ANTHONY: No, it comes back. You can see the difference between the two: what has been given to you by the higher Self and how the ego usurps that. The very first thing that you'll say is, "*I* had the experience." Right away the ego gets intothe act.

There are many good examples. You can make a study of some of these preachers that have a million-dollar radio station and a five-million-dollar stadium in which to announce their "startling" discoveries.

One of the things you'll notice is that usually these people are more or less affirming the ego, not denying it. If you listen to them carefully, they're always in the process of affirming their ego.

JNL: When you have a mystical experience, how do you differentiate between the phony illumination and the real?

ANTHONY: One of the basics, I would say, is a feeling of humility. If that's not there, then be suspicious.

But we don't want to get into criteria right now as to what is authentic experience and what is non-authentic. What we want to understand is that the ego has enough craftiness to create divergences or side issues and have you follow them up and, as it goes along, even to bring about a reaffirmation that what it is doing is spiritually correct. In most of the cases, you're going to have to use your reasoning.

You'll taste it. The ego has a very peculiar flavor. You can recognize it—if you have any self-awareness, that is.

AH: Is this path that aggrandizes the ego a standard situation?

ANTHONY: Oh yes, sure.

AH: Everyone who gets interested in the path has to be interested via the ego.

ANTHONY: Yes, it's true for everyone that it's through the ego that we become interested in these things. But it would follow that if a person's sincere, he can see the phoniness, he can see when he's being phony.

AH: Is understanding this quote a prerequisite to going on the quest?

ANTHONY: You could be on the quest and the ego could take you right off it, too. It can supply you with all the necessary ingredients to make you think you *are* on the quest.

AH: It would seem that there is an attitude of ambition that would point to the ego in regard to spiritual things.

ANTHONY: Yes, but don't restrict it to ambition. It would vary with individuals.

WITHIN his heart, he may call or keep nothing as his own, not even his spirituality. If he really does not want to cling to the ego, he must cling to nothing else. He is to have no sense of inner greatness, no distinct feeling of having attained some high degree of holiness.

(V12, 18:4.140 AND *Perspectives*, P. 225)

ANTHONY: As soon as you say you're spiritual, the ego has taken over.

To GIVE UP the ego is to refuse to accept its dominance or to acquiesce in its thought. It is to regard the ego as the shadow masquerading as the light. But the mere holding of such a view does not result in the dismissal of the ego. For that, a long course of preparation and training and labor and discipline is required. This course is what we know as the Quest. To give up the ego one must begin by hating it, one must go on through an incessant struggle against it, and one must end by overcoming it.

The aspirant must train himself to view his thoughts in the proper perspective, refusing to regard their insistent attractions and repulsions as his own. He must cultivate the habit of being an observer of his own thoughts and activities in the same objective way that he observes strangers in the street. He must regard himself with detachment and his experiences with calm, if he is to arrive at the truth of the one and learn the lessons of the other. While he clings to the possessive little ego, he clings also to fears and anxieties, discords and despair. He gets too emotionally involved in his personal problems and so obscures true issues, or distorts or magnifies them.

However much a man may wish to free himself from the tyranny of the ego, he finds that wishing alone does not do it for him, aspiration alone cannot achieve it for him. It is because of this weakness of human nature, due to the age-old character of the ego's life, that the training and discipline and the practices of the Quest have been instituted. Through them he may be able to achieve what wishing alone is unable to accomplish.

(FIRST AND THIRD PARAGRAPHS PREVIOUSLY
UNPUBLISHED. SECOND APPEARS IN
Essays on the Quest, P. 189.)

EC: It seems like the ego has to be built up to some degree to be able to approach the quest, doesn't it?

ANTHONY: Yes, that's what we refer to as the mental perfection of the ego, the mental development of the ego.[1]

AH: So one aspect of this training is the continual attempt to observe one's own motivations and actions in the same kind of dispassionate way that you can observe a stranger's. I'm still looking for a way of validating this alleged objective experience that we're always having. What criterion do we have?

ANTHONY: There are a couple of ways. One way is speaking to a teacher or someone you regard as a friend in spiritual matters. Another way is to watch the consequences; that's always very revealing. A third is to use your reason, common sense.

But basically a teacher will tell you. He might not put it very bluntly, it depends on the teacher. He might say, "Well, that's not really the way it is, it's the other way." You may come out of mystical experience with a vision that you are the new messiah, and someone has to put you in your place. Now, you can go the hard way, you can go out with a sign and say, "The world's ending tomorrow," and walk in front of the White House, or you can listen when your teacher says, "Well, that's just the ego interpreting the experience that it has and it got very inflated." The ego will be right there, right alongside the spiritual experience misinterpreting it, don't worry. You'll find out.

VM: Here's one to support what you're saying.

THE STUDENT must beware of the cunning disguises of the retreating ego. He must beware of its self-flattery pretending to be the Overself's flattery. He must beware of any "mission" to which he is appointed. If the inner voice promises him a remarkable future, whether a spiritual attainment or a worldly triumph, disbelieve it. Only if it makes him humbler and meeker should he believe it.   (*Essays on the Quest,* P. 185)

ANTHONY: That's even a better criterion, isn't it? Makes you humbler: That's the criterion.

AH: If it leads to a situation of humility, at least you know the ego isn't taking over.

NH: We were talking about seeing the ego's functioning objectively, and I'm wondering if just by seeing it, it becomes available.

ANTHONY: By "seeing," do you know what is meant? Maybe we should ask what we mean by "seeing."

HS: I would say you mean a *seeing through* to the actual meaning/knowledge present in an event.

ANTHONY: "Seeing through" is good. In the epistemological relationship you have the object, the subject, and the seeing. You notice the strange thing about *seeing*—"seeing" includes both the subject and the object. If you don't see that way, you haven't seen. It's just the ego functioning. Follow? By "seeing," that's what *I* mean—I don't know what you mean. If you say, "I see something," that's not the seeing that's going to bring about the detached, impersonal objectivity that we are calling for. When the ego sees something, you do not have detachment, objectivity. It's only "seeing" that will show that the ego as a subject and the object that it claims to perceive are two sides of the same coin.

HS: And you said before it doesn't have a mode, it's non-modal?

ANTHONY: That *seeing* is non-modal. It's neither subjective nor objective.

AH: Is that seeing a rare occurrence in our experience?

ANTHONY: It's not that rare, but it depends. Again, it's a general question. I can't answer it. You'd have to tell me who you're referring to.

AH: Are you equating that seeing with *satori*?

ANTHONY: Yes, it can be a *satori*. It can also be an insightful moment in the daily life. Don't make these things so mysterious and religious and put monk's robes on them and have temples built. They go on all the time!

AH: It just seems to me, Anthony, that any objectification of that ego is not a very normal sort of occurrence.

ANTHONY: Yes.

AH: But we seem to be talking about it as if it happens maybe once or twice a week.

ANTHONY: *It might if you listen! It might even happen once or twice a day!* Why are you trying to quantify what I'm saying? These things happen. I'm just trying to make it as prosaic as possible so that you stop thinking that it belongs somewhere in the Himalayas. I'm talking about what is going on all the time. You don't have to be a genius like Einstein and have the theory of relativity. Why do you people insist on making these things so mysterious?

AH: It's just that on the one hand we speak of this ego as being such a . . .

ANTHONY: So clever, yes. And on the other hand, it happens, it happens. And it's better that you keep a positive outlook about these things.

EC: Non-modal seeing—isn't that the higher "I"?

ANTHONY: Sure it's the higher "I." But now you already put up a roadblock, "It's the higher 'I,' it won't happen to me. Let me get back to my ego way." It's just like when I used to say that you think hardness into existence, and someone used to say, "Me? I do no such thing! " Let's resume.

ALL YOUR THINKING about the ego is necessarily incomplete, for it does not include the ego-thought itself. Try to do so, and it slips from your hold. Only something that transcends the ego can grasp it.

(v6, 8:2.66 AND *Perspectives*, P. 96)

ANTHONY: So basically we would say that within the

structure of the ego complex you cannot grasp it. At the very most you would get an aspect of the way it functions, but you wouldn't be able to grasp the ego-thought itself because you have to step outside of that.

RC: You can read descriptions of your psyche's structure inside the ego but you can't *see* inside.

ANTHONY: Because you're *inside* doing that. You have to get outside. And that means that you'd have to identify with the calmness or the stillness, right? But who wants to be calm and still when we could have so much agitation and activity going on up there?

AH: Is it appropriate to say "I am calm?"

ANTHONY: No, because then you're agitated. If you say anything you've already produced all the agitation you need.

THE EGOIST has as much chance of finding real peace
of mind as the historian has of finding truth in politics.

(v6, 8:3.150)

HS: OK, but would you say that "calm abiding" is the mode that you use?

ANTHONY: If you want to know the ego.

HS: There's no other way you could ever gain any sort of knowledge of it?

ANTHONY: What he's saying there is that the ego itself cannot be known from within the ego.

RG: It can only be known from that calmness.

ANTHONY: From outside.

RG: From the calmness it can be seen as an object. The whole subject-object situation is known.

ANTHONY: In other words, the ego and its image-activity, its imaginal activity, are both present. Instead of saying subject and object, say the ego and its image-activity. The activity of the ego is to make images.

AH: That's present.

ANTHONY: That would be present while you're still. Because if you're still, if you're calm, then you are the higher consciousness.

AH: That presence is not to be construed as any kind of dualistic circumstance. It's not like you have a higher subject and a higher object.

ANTHONY: No, it isn't that you have a higher subject and a higher object. It isn't like that at all.

AH: That would be logically impossible.

ANTHONY: Because then you can go on doing that forever.

DD: Is it a seeing that disturbs calmness?

ANTHONY: No, it's a seeing in the way I used the term seeing which includes subject-object relationships. And that seeing is very calm. There's no agitation because it's not a seeing on the part of the ego. It's not a seeing that the ego has. When they say the *prajna*-eye [wisdom-eye] sees, you're not to think of another eye in the middle of your head looking out at the ego and its world. It's seeing in the sense that we spoke about before, that subsumes both and includes them within itself.

UNTIL IT IS brought to his attention, he may not know that the idol at whose feet he is continually worshipping is the ego. If he could give to God the same amount of remembrance that he gives to his ego, he could quite soon attain, and become established in, that enlightenment to which other men devote lifetimes of arduous effort. (v6, 8:4.153)

LR: What does it mean to remember God?

PD: Forget yourself.

ANTHONY: When you sit down to meditate—or you don't even have to sit down to meditate, but just watch your mind—there's an almost incessant chattering going on.

Thought follows upon thought, endlessly. These thoughts are usually about something from your past—some pleasant memory or occasion—or some expectation, but it will always be about yourself.

And you say to yourself, "I've had enough of this. I don't want to listen to this fellow any more." You become very determined that every time an idea or thought or memory—whatever—springs up, you will resolutely push it out. Now if you do that, that's equivalent to showing and expressing, *in act*, your faith in the Higher. But every time that a thought comes into your mind and you give it heed, then you are expressing faith in the lower self, and you believe in your ego.

Like a thought, a memory comes up: "Oh, twelve years ago on a certain day I had this beautiful occasion. Somebody gave me $150 and I had a good day . . ." and so on. That memory will come up, and you'll look at it: "Yeah, yeah, yeah, sure. I remember." Well, as all these images keep coming up, they suck your attention—there's a preoccupation with them. You could refer to the totality of all these images as what is known. And you could see that it's faith in the lower self that you're expressing.

But if you deny these things, if you do not let them come in, if every time a thought arises in your mind you cut off its head—you cut it right off—then you're expressing faith in the Higher. That's a real remembrance of the Higher. Try for an hour or ten minutes, five minutes. Try it. And see who you believe.

AH: So by rejecting the lower, you don't replace it with thoughts of the Higher.

ANTHONY: No. Just reject the lower; don't replace it with more thoughts, because they too will be known. Forget about yourself, and that will be the remembrance. This, of course, is something you have to practice, not talk about.

Now that doesn't mean that if you have a problem you

shouldn't work out the problem; it requires your attention. So there shouldn't be any reason for a person to excuse himself. "Well, I forgot to pay the rent, I didn't think about it." We're not talking about that. Those things that require your thought have to be given thought, but once done: over with it.

You'll see that the negatives are basically an expression of the ego. The ego could always keep you preoccupied with itself through the negative emotions. See, by sending this smoke screen up, it keeps you preoccupied with itself. All the time, all you're thinking about is "me, me, me, me." As a matter of fact, there's a lovely cartoon. It showed a door—like the president of the bank has his name on the door—well, this fellow only had the word "Me." Me, me, me! [*laughter*]

LG: This is very different from the practice of the presence of God that Brother Lawrence talks about.

ANTHONY: He eventually would have to stop practicing the presence of God by thought. This is very direct. You don't substitute good thoughts for bad thoughts, because you want to get rid of thoughts, period—good or bad. You just want to get rid of thoughts. All thought will constantly preoccupy you with itself, and the ego will have its way. That's the way the ego keeps you under its thumb. But once you decide to start struggling with your thoughts, you've got a conflict, a long one.

In many of the Japanese paintings of Zen masters they have the Zen master sitting with a stick. That's to chase away the thoughts. It's not to hit people with.

You get the opportunity every day when you sit down to meditate. You see the thoughts that come up into your mind and you see how they preoccupy you and how they keep you away from what you want to do. That's why meditation always, in the beginning phases, is so painful; it's a constant struggle with these thoughts.

It is so difficult to believe that something so flimsy, so invisible and intangible as the thoughts that we have, can keep us in bondage forever. You would expect big chains wrapped around you—that's going to keep you in bondage. No, it's much subtler. It's just thoughts; every thought we have is like a nail on the box.

> TAKE IT AS a truism that nearly every man is in love with himself . . .

ANTHONY: That's an axiom.

> . . . If the divine influence is to enter and touch him, much more if it is to possess him, he must be deprived of this self-love.   (v6, 8:3.134)

EM: It's interesting, because it seems like you have to be deprived of your self-hate as well.

ANTHONY: Well, I don't think he means self-love and self-hate in that sense. He's not talking about the opposites here when he says self-love. It's built into the very nature of the ego that it cannot consider anyone else. That I-ness, that self-infatuation, that self-conceit is not something other than the ego; it *is* the ego. So how could you possibly get rid of it? By hating it? That shows just another way of loving it. Because if you're going to be attached to it you've got something there to hate so you'll be preoccupied with it. If you love it, then you're still preoccupied with it. So it's not at that level. It's something much deeper than that.[2]

As a matter of fact, a person is not truly and really on the quest until he has that self-hate, until he sees the ego as what it is: *his worst enemy*. There couldn't be a worse enemy. But to see that, you have to be ready, because the world is going to have to come in and really deal you a crushing blow, one way or another. You remember the old saying, "When the heart is broken, then Christ can come in." It's some sort of situation like that. The world—or some situation, or circumstances, or events—just comes in and shatters you, and in that moment you can see what the ego is really like because you've been humiliated. It won't last very long, believe me, because the ego will come around picking up the pieces and putting them together right away. But at that instant, it would be enough to see that that's who your enemy is. That's what has to be overcome.

And that's what I think the Buddha was referring to when he said that a man who conquers a thousand men a thousand times is not as great as the man who has conquered himself. The man who has conquered himself has overcome that self-conceit, has seen into the very nature of his ego and overcome it.

They have a lot of stories and tales about that. The dweller at the threshold is supposed to be like an amalgamation of your past, and this picture that is presented is like a picture or a summary of what your ego is like. And I don't know of anyone who has ever found the so-called "dweller" very handsome or alluring. They've usually been frightened by it.

So basically we have to understand that the self-conceit that's built into the very nature of the ego is difficult to get rid of. The ego reaches a point where it recognizes that it is itself its own worst enemy. Now what do you do? You wait.

THE READINESS to surrender his lower nature to the higher one, to give up his own will in obedience to God's will, to put aside the ego for the sake of the Overself, puts a man far in advance of his fellows, but it also puts him into certain dangers and misconceptions of its own. The first danger is that he has given up his own will only to obey other men's wills, surrendered his own ego only to fall under the influence of other men's egos. The first misconception is to take lesser voices for

God's voice. The second danger is to fall into personal
idleness under the illusion that it is mystical passivity.
The second misconception is to forget that although
self-efforts are not enough of themselves to guarantee
the oncoming of Grace, they are still necessary prerequisites to that oncoming. His intellectual, emotional, and
moral disciplines are as needed to attract that Grace as
are his aspirations, yearnings, and prayers for it. He
cannot expect God to do for him work which should be
done by himself.   (v6, 8:4.210)

ANTHONY: So what does it mean to give up the self-will? I
hope you don't think of it as something that you could do
with one stroke. To give up the self-will is to no longer allow
or permit the lower mind or the lower self to perpetually occupy you with its own thoughts.

AH: How does enthusiasm for being on the quest separate
itself from self-will?

ANTHONY: Well, you had the enthusiasm when you first
went on the quest, right? You wanted to get on with the
quest. And one of the things that's required to get on with the
quest is to give up the self-will or the preoccupation with the
lower self. You're actually doing it when you're involved in
this particular effort.

But again, as I pointed out, it doesn't mean that you have
to become myopic or intellectually blind. You can see what's
going on. As a matter of fact, you'll probably see better
what's going on when you stop *reacting* to what's going on.
You're of the opinion that a reaction is required in order for
you to proceed on the quest.

AH: A self-effort is required.

ANTHONY: Well, yes, you're making the effort insofar as
you're keeping the lower thoughts at a distance. But the
point I'm getting to is that—again, I'll repeat—you're of the

opinion that a reaction is required on your part in order to get on with the quest. "You have to be enthusiastic, you have to know what you're doing." These are all reactions. If you keep the thoughts at a distance and you prevent them from coming in, you'll also get guidance.

I think we should dwell just a moment or two on that notion of the self-will. Examine it. What does it mean?

AH: If there's one who's acting, then it's self-will.

ANTHONY: Yes. Let's try being very practical, all right? You get up, you have your breakfast, you go to work. Most of these duties are prescribed. But what we're talking about here is that what accompanies them is unnecessary—the constant series of reactions to every little incident that occurs in your life. You get up in the morning, and you've had toast for ten years. This morning, you react to toast, "Well, I didn't cover that piece of toast with the butter!" Just watch the numberless thoughts that are absolutely irrelevant and utterly meaningless and worthless. You can live your life very perfectly without them.

If we start right there, just at that level, does that mean that you're not going to go to school and start teaching or do whatever chores are required? Can't you carry wood, so to speak, or chop it and carry water without all those thoughts?

AH: Yes.

ANTHONY: But have you noticed the occasion where you chop wood and carry water and you didn't have the thoughts?

RG: How would you notice?

ANTHONY: Oh, you'll notice. Your mind will be quieter. You won't be always agitated, restless, going to Florida, or Labrador, or Greenland, or wherever you can go. You can take most of the mental activity that goes on in your life during the day and chuck ninety percent out the window and be so much the better for it.

AH: It seems that much of that useless activity is oriented towards *my* preferences.

ANTHONY: Yes, there's always the "I" behind it. But notice the tremendous psychical dissipation that's going on. It's like you've left the electricity on, and you don't need to. You're just wasting it. It's a dissipation that comes through extroversion and goes on all the time.

The thing has to be practiced to be appreciated, and then a lot of the questions, which are really theoretical, get answered in the very doing of it. It's not going to stop you from doing the things you have to do. Let's say you're building something and you've got to make plans—we're not talking about not thinking there. You can see that it's a thinking that's attached to a very specific object; you're trying to make a door, you're measuring it, you have to think, "Well, let's see. Two times two is twenty-four; two times two is . . . no, *four!*" You have to think, sure!

Dropping the irrelevant thoughts is part of the way we gradually learn to surrender our self-will. It isn't a dramatic event that all at once you give up your self-will and say, "Well, I gave it up." It works in this very slow way: Every time you turn out a thought or you refuse to give it recognition, you're giving up something of your self-will. In other words, if I'm irritated, and I feel like saying, "You . . ." and I *don't* do it. And there's nothing wrong with suppressing these things. Don't let the analysts scare you; there's nothing wrong with saying, "I'm *not* going to do that, period." Because it's right on the stage, the stage of your consciousness, it's illuminated —it won't be a repression.

As a matter of fact, it will be something worse than a repression. It will be an open conflict. "You're not going to have your way. Out!" And every time a negative emotion comes up and wants to express itself and you refuse to acknowledge it, well, that's a little bit of surrendering of self-will. Every time you refuse to acknowledge what the lower self wants you to do or wants you to think or wants you to feel, you are surrendering that self-will.

And now your comment is going to be, "This seems like you have to make an effort, that you have to apply the will." Yes, you have to apply the will to get rid of the will, but then you get rid of both of them, because it will be as automatic a habit as any other habit. But if you believe that it's going to be an application of will, and now you see a logical contradiction in it, that'll save you the trouble of trying it out.

I just want you to understand: I'm thinking of self-will at this very practical, everyday, every-moment level. I'm not thinking of being hung up on a cross and saying, "I'll give up my will." I'm thinking of this every moment, moment by moment, life. Let's reread the quote a few lines at a time.

THE READINESS to surrender his lower nature to the higher one, to give up his own will in obedience to God's will, to put aside the ego for the sake of the Overself, puts a man far in advance of his fellows, but it also puts him into certain dangers and misconceptions of its own. The first danger is that he has given up his own will only to obey other men's wills, surrendered his own ego only to fall under the influence of other men's egos. The first misconception is to take lesser voices for God's voice. . . .

ANTHONY: You may intellectually understand what I say; but if you have not perceived it, you have not grasped my meaning. When a person actually perceives, perceives the way this process is constantly involving you in what we call life and death, the everyday world, then there is no choice. It isn't a question of will. You just don't want to go that way. No will: You just say, "I see that's not the way."

Now, it is a habit. It will persist. It will constantly keep occurring. Instant by instant thoughts will keep coming up. But something in you has changed; something in you has turned away from that. That's what I mean when I say you "perceive" this. It isn't just understood intellectually. Because you won't do it from the point of view of just intellectually understanding something. You know, you can understand intellectually that "honesty is the best policy," but you won't *do* it. In the same way, this thing could be understood intellectually, but until it's perceived as the actual mental processes that are involving you in this constant state of inner agitation and pain—until then, you won't do it.

When you do see it—I won't say it's effortless, because the habit will persist—but then there arises from this knowledge the need not to give heed any more to that lower self. So I could interpret it that way: that it's the result of a true perception, true understanding. And then the person just can't help but ignore the thoughts as they keep coming at him.

It's like sometimes when you've seen a picture twenty times: You just don't want to look at it any more. You're bored. It's just so meaningless.

I think you have the experience when you sit down and you just meditate, and you watch the thoughts. They'll be the same now as they were ten years ago or will be ten years from now. They'll be the same merry-go-round.

AH: This perception that you describe is not intellectual.

ANTHONY: Well, it's more than intellectual. It's not that it's not intellectual; it's a little bit more than intellectual.

AH: I was wondering if that's equivalent to the Buddhist idea of revulsion.

ANTHONY: Yes.

AH: Where one experiences a revulsion of one's self?

ANTHONY: *Paravritti*, is that what they call it? They speak about it in the *Lankavatara Sutra*. And you have to work very hard to bring that moment of revulsion which is like a 180-degree turn away from yourself. But for the person that has experienced revulsion, it doesn't mean that the thoughts have stopped. You'll see that they'll still continuously be regurgitating the past, because it's a machine. It just keeps going.

There are enough references in [D.T.] Suzuki about that revulsion, and how hard you have to work to get it. Because if it's just an intellectual insight, you won't do it. It's a turning about, 180 degrees.

NG: What would it mean to work very hard for that?

ANTHONY: Try to see it for yourself. You have to constantly turn your eye inward to try to catch the mind doing these things. And that means that there has to be almost a microscopic scrutiny going on all the time. Now, you may not succeed all the time, but one instant you may, and you suddenly see that. And you see that this is the way the mind is constantly working. This is a *real seeing*. It's when you're not thinking, you're not making any kind of judgements, you have no mind-set, anything like that—at that instant, you may see it, and it will bring about a kind of revulsion.

Take an instance where a person enjoys doing something very much. After that revulsion takes place, he may go on doing it, but the desire to do so has been cut away. That's not there; that's not compulsively binding him to it. So they work very hard to bring about this state.

But, nonetheless, the important thing here is to bring it down to this very practical level, where every instant you look at your mind, and you keep watching your mind, and you keep trying to eliminate the thoughts that come to it. You keep doing that. That's a kind of preparation for it. The revulsion might come that way. There's tremendous difficulty in trying to predict what the result of any spiritual discipline is. It may never be what you set out to do.

> [*re-reading continues*] . . . The second danger is to fall
> into personal idleness under the illusion that it is
> mystical passivity. The second misconception is to
> forget that although self-efforts are not enough of

themselves to guarantee the oncoming of Grace, they
are still necessary prerequisites to that oncoming . . .

ANTHONY: PB keeps those two things in balance: You
have to make the effort to keep the thoughts out, but at the
same time there should always be an aspiration towards the
Higher. They have to be kept in balance. It's not enough just
to keep pushing the thoughts out. Every now and then prayer,
worship, devotion for the Higher, and aspiration also have to
find a root, have to find a place. And these two things together
make it possible, as he says, for an influx of grace to occur.
You cannot force grace, but, on the other hand, it can't come
as long as you're always preoccupied with your business or
your farm or whatever preoccupation you may have. It can't
come in.

RC: Suppose I take the attitude that I'm not going to have
any thoughts—I take the perspective of the will. It seems I can
do that as an exercise for a certain length of time in meditation. But it also seems that some of these thoughts that are
imposed on me are imposed because I really do need to attend
to the things that they're hounding me about. There are certain thoughts that I can't keep out because there are certain
changes in me that are required, and those thoughts are
making me aware of that.

ANTHONY: I have to pay my electric bill, and tomorrow I'll
sign a check and put it in the envelope. And as I sign the
check—and let's say it's $128—I don't have to say, "This is a
rip-off!" I do have to sign the check; I do have to mail them
the money that they have coming to them, and I could do that
without all the extraneous matters: "This is a rip-off; the util-
ity companies are robbing us left and right, and I know the
chairman, and he's living in the lap of luxury . . ." and that can
go on and on. You do have to sign the check; you do have
to think, "I've got to sign the check and I've got to mail the

letter." The rest is not necessary.

I'm telling you: Your workload will be reduced by about eighty-five percent, just in terms of the psychical energy that you have at your disposal. You have to understand that as soon as I say, "It's a rip-off," that's a reaction. And the whole of the organism, with all its memories, is involved. That keeps the ego in control, as soon as there's the slightest reaction.

AH: You're suggesting that's an appropriate attitude towards all possible thoughts.

ANTHONY: You have to think thoughts at certain times. For instance when we're discussing certain ideas, we have to think. I'm just suggesting that there is an approach to life where the necessary things that have to be done can be done, and the extraneous reactions and considerations can be left alone, left aside. There's no way I can convince you except for you to try it.

RC: We're talking about trying to undermine the self-will. Some of these thoughts—entertaining them, reflecting on them—are also effective in undermining self-will.

ANTHONY: Yes, because there you're not preoccupied with the ego and its problems. If I'm trying to understand the nature of something, I'm certainly not preoccupied with the kind of contents that the ego would be interested in.

> [*re-reading continues*] . . . His intellectual, emotional,
> and moral disciplines are as needed to attract that Grace
> as are his aspirations, yearnings, and prayers for it. He
> cannot expect God to do for him work which should be
> done by himself.

ANTHONY: And what do you think it is that you have to do for yourself that He won't do for you? Refrain from thinking. You have to look a thought right in the face and see it for what it is, and you'll see a hydra-headed beast hidden in it.

We're hypnotized by thought, and we think it's something worth looking at. But someday you'll see that thought—you know the way a snake hypnotizes a bird?—has one function, to hypnotize you, to make sure you don't get anywhere near reality or even think about reality. That's its preoccupation.

All thinking is self-willing. That's the whole point. Certainly when I pay my electric bill, it isn't that kind of self-willing. That's not involved. But as soon as the thought comes, "You remember you had coffee with that beautiful dame the other day?"—that's self-willing. Thought is willing itself. And you have to see it; you actually have to see it. Until you do see it, thought will always exercise its endearment, its glamour, and hypnotize you. Every now and then, stop and look at your mind and you'll see the way you've been hypnotized for an hour or so with all kinds of thoughts.

RC: I was trying to put the success or failure that one has with that exercise into the context of one's whole life. One's whole life may be such that he or she cannot succeed at that exercise until certain changes are made.

ANTHONY: Perhaps we could put what you're saying this way. Is there a series of intermediate steps that leads up to this recognition and which you have to make note of as you're going along? Before the arisal of this moment of perception which we're calling revulsion, there are certain things about my character or characteristics that I work with that have to be made available to me. And these glimpses into my own psychology will eventually provide a sufficient scaffolding on which or by which the revulsion can happen. The revulsion doesn't occur out of the blue. There was a series of steps leading up to it, whether we consciously or unconsciously recognized these steps that led to that position.

One might notice, for instance, at various times in his life a certain disgust or nausea overcoming him, and he traces it to its origins psychologically. He recognizes something about the almost monotonous repetition that is going on in our daily lives and which we consider to be so important. A few of these recognitions will eventually help a person to struggle to get to the insight or the understanding of what revulsion is. We've all at times had that experience where we get nauseated; we've done something so many times that it's lost its novelty, its glamour; it's become meaningless. This is like a little taste of what that revulsion is.

The other thing: I'm a fanatic. Once you sit down to meditate, take out your sword or your battle-axe or your mace, whatever you've got, and no matter what it is, no matter how glorious the intuition, cut it off. You must be a fanatic when you sit down, up to a certain point. After that, the intuitions will tell you what to do.

> THERE WOULD BE no hope of ever getting out of this ego-centered position if we did not know these three things. First, the ego is only an accumulation of memories and a series of cravings, that is, thought; it is a fictitious entity. Second, the thinking activity can come to an end in stillness. Third, Grace, the radiation of the Power beyond man, is ever-shining and ever-present. If we let the mind become deeply still and deeply observant of the ego's self-preserving instinct, we open the door to Grace, which then lovingly swallows us.
>
> (v6, 8:4.417)

ANTHONY: So if we think about it, did you ever experience that the whole of the perceived world is like one huge prison? The blue sky and the white clouds and the bosom of the earth, the flatness that goes on as far as the horizon, did you ever experience that as bondage, as being a prison? It's strange.

Some people would say, "How could you feel like a prisoner? You look out, and there's thousands of miles in front of you." But one experiences it as if he's enclosed in a circle of thoughts that he can't get out of. That's why he experiences a certain bondage. The bondage is to these thoughts, the circle of thoughts. He may not be able to explain it intellectually, but that's what's going on. He's a prisoner of his own thoughts.

Then the second thing PB says is that mind can be brought to a point of cessation. Another way of looking at it would be to say, "Mind doesn't have to think these thoughts! If mind doesn't have to think these thoughts, then I'll be free."

EM: No matter how many times you say that, it's hard to imagine.

ANTHONY: I know; you cannot imagine it, because thought cannot conceive its own cessation. That's out of the question. But we could try to make a leap and use an analogy.

You have a dream and you're in the dream and you know that everything that you're perceiving in the dream is nothing but a cluster of thoughts, sensations, but somehow you're locked into it, you can't get out. And then the dream character finds a book in the dream library and the book tells him that the master stroke is to stop the mind from thinking. So the dream character sits down and says, "I'm going to meditate; I'm going to stop thinking." So he stops thinking and the dream disappears! There are no thoughts any more; he's not thinking, so he momentarily experiences freedom. Then thought resumes and he's back in jail again, but he's witnessed the fact that thought is what imprisons us. Cessation of thought is what frees us.

The third step is the radiation of Grace. That's very difficult because that's like saying, "When we are free, when we experience ourselves free of body, free of mind, then the 'you' that's there experiences a certain Grace which is from the soul— altogether different." I don't want to go into the third one.

But those are three important points to remember. First,

thought imprisons us. Secondly, since thought is the product of thinking, and one can learn to cease thinking by having thinking thinking about itself, then the way out is found. Just like when we said thoughts are coming into your mind, and I tell you, "Don't identify with them. Don't give them any attention. They'll die." At the moment that you stop giving them attention, it's like you're making an attempt to cease thinking, and you get out of that bondage to these thoughts that are trying to suck you in and say, "Here I am! Identify with me and you'll be happy."

BS: Can Grace give you an insight into the reality of the world?

ANTHONY: It can. It can take that form; it could take many forms. That's one form it takes; it shows the unreality of the thoughts that we live within.

It takes a little Grace for this understanding to occur, to recognize that we are imprisoned within our own thought. It may take a little Grace to understand that, or to understand that perception, insofar as it comports possession, limits the person to his possessions, binds him hand and foot to these possessions, and so he's not free. Do you see what I'm saying? That perception could actually limit your infinite freedom.

We have the interesting example of Krishnamurti when he had a moment of the experience of being without body and mind, when he thought he was going to pass out. For most people it would be that kind of a thing, where if the body and mind are taken away, then the person temporarily swoons or passes out, doesn't know what's going on. But after that, Grace will show them the way further on. Of these three important points, it's the first two that we're concerned about. The third one takes care of itself.

LR: Are you equating perception with the thoughts of the ego?

ANTHONY: No, I think I would say perception, the way I

generally use it and even now, belongs to the epistemological subject.

LR: So one could still have perception and experience the consciousness which is the Overself?

ANTHONY: Yes. You have to remember that this is just an analogy or an example. It occasionally occurs to people that the world is stale, flat, and a nuisance. You must have had the experience that everything just felt worthless. There is an experience, right there, where the person is feeling the bondage of thought. He knows in his heart that he's in prison. That was the point of the analogy.

BS: The other side, of course, is the stillness. Not being in bondage would be freedom. The stillness would be the freedom.

ANTHONY: The stillness could be right there in the perception. That's the point she [LR] wanted to make, but I just wanted to make it simpler by separating the two things.

FD: Can the ego be equated with perception?

ANTHONY: They are not equatable, but they're concomitant. You're not going to have one without the other.

FD: They're not the same?

ANTHONY: No. Otherwise your language wouldn't be able to hold up any distinction between the perceived world and the ego. When you say ego, you don't mean the perceived world, do you? And when you speak about the perceived world you don't mean the ego, but you know that they're concomitant. You're not going to have one without the other.

[*Quote is re-read*]

ANTHONY: The Mind is whole and undivided, and before it gets divided you don't have those things like instinct, self-preservation; none of that exists. As soon as the Mind divides itself into thinker and thought, then all those things come into existence, all those things come into being. So if you could stand at the point where the Mind is whole, undivided, you're outside that conflict. That's why it's so important to try to cultivate a quiet mind, because a quiet mind is a mind that's whole and undivided and isn't preoccupied, so to speak, with the thoughts of the ego. There it stands, prior to the part of itself that identifies with the body. And in that identification with the body's sensation, it thinks itself as the body.

Of course, that's what all the great teachers hammer away at. Try to get to the quiet mind, the mind that *is* when thinking ceases. And if thinking inquires into its own nature, it is eventually forced into that position where it's quiet. It actually ceases functioning when it tries to understand its own nature. And at that moment, like he said, it's like before being embodied.

But you see, we're talking about very practical things now. We're talking about what has to be done every day.

CDA: When you say that thinking has to understand its own nature, is that the same as what you called "perceiving"?

ANTHONY: It's a little bit different. There wouldn't be any perception there. It would be more the nature of an intuition. When the thinking principle inquires into its own nature and tries to confront it, it's reduced to silence. Then an intuition arises. That wouldn't be a perception, whereas what we were speaking about before was an actual perception of the way the mind functions. The way the mind functions can be perceived, but when we speak about the undivided Mind, there's no functioning there. There's nothing to perceive there; you can only intuit that.

CDA: When you say "the thinking principle inquires into itself," what do you mean by the thinking principle there?

ANTHONY: I mean thinking, the thinking in you that's constantly going on.

CDA: The thinking of the empirical ego that's going on?

ANTHONY: No, the thinking is going to *produce* the empirical ego.

Just drop it away. Just stop for a minute. You know that you are a thinking being. You're not going to be preoccupied with the external world; you're not going to be preoccupied with the internal images or pictures. Thinking is going to be preoccupied with itself, and only itself. Now, if you proceed by this method, eventually what happens is that thinking halts; thinking ceases. You get quiet. Because there is no answer to that.

Now, that cannot be a perception. It's closer to a feeling, an intuition. "Ah! This is what I am: I'm mind." Now, of course you can see that's wrong; you can't say that because that's a thought. Whereas when I tell a person, "Try to perceive the fact that the mind is constantly creating," that can be done.

It's something like this. Let's say I know I dream. Now, could I stand outside and watch the mind making the dream? That would be a perception. You'd have to actually perceive the way the mind is weaving all these things together and projecting an image. That can be perceived; the other thing cannot be perceived.

When we do the next meditation retreat, I want you to be so fed up with your ego that you're actually going to say, "I don't want you around, brother. Scram!" And he'll come back twice as strong. As soon as I started increasing my meditations to four and five a day, I started getting wobbly knees, broken ankles, stupid inflammation of the nerves—everything comes out. The ego's right there, pitching in: "I'm going to stop this guy, no matter what." [laughs]

AP: It must be possible to have a still mind even though the body is disturbing.

ANTHONY: Yes. Of course. Otherwise it wouldn't be worth very much! If I can only have a still mind when I'm sitting still, and then the body moves around and . . . No! The ideal is to have a still mind even when you're in the midst of a lot of trouble—I mean, activity! [*laughter*]

There's a beautiful statement where PB says, "Be calm. Make that your talisman." No matter what, be calm. When they invest the Brahmin with the thread, isn't that the only advice they give him? "Be calm."³

AP: Can this calmness include even a disturbed mind? Can it be there in the depths, even though your surface mind is not still?

ANTHONY: Sure, it's always there as the background. The surface mind could be noisy, and that could be quiet, and you could see that your mind is noisy and agitated. And usually when you recognize the fact that you're in a state of agitation, it's information coming to you from the quiet part, telling you, "Look at that! It's a real burlesque going on."

CDA: It's peculiar to me that you could have a quiet mind and the quiet mind can perceive all the noise that's going on.

ANTHONY: Of course it's preferable not to have the noise going on.

CDA: So the fact that it is not a constant state does not negate the awareness of the wholeness of the mind.

ANTHONY: It is a constant state, but there are four levels to that state. There's quiet mind one, quiet mind two, quiet mind three, and there's *really* quiet mind.

CDA: So this is "quiet mind one"?

ANTHONY: Yes. We're satisfied with that. If we get that, we'll say, "OK for this life!"

There's a quote where PB speaks about a dirty window. You clean it a little bit, and that's the first level of the quiet mind. And then you clean it very well—second level of quiet mind entered.

THERE ARE varying degrees of spiritual illumination, which accounts both for the varying outlooks to be found among mystics and for the different kinds of

Glimpse among aspirants. All illuminations and all
Glimpses free the man from his negative qualities and
base nature, but in the latter case only temporarily. He is
able, as a result, to see into his higher nature. In the first
degree, it is as if a window covered with dirt were
cleaned enough to reveal a beautiful garden outside it.
He is still subject to the activity of thinking, the emotion of joy, and the discrimination between X and Y. In
the next and higher degree, it is as if the window were
still more cleaned so that still more beauty is revealed
beyond it. Here there are no thoughts to intervene
between the seer and the seen. In the third degree, the
discrimination is no longer present. In the fourth
degree, it as as if the window were thoroughly cleaned.
Here there is no longer even a rapturous emotion but
only a balanced happiness, a steady tranquillity which,
being beyond the intellect, cannot properly be described
by the intellect.

Again, mental peace is a fruit of the first and lowest
degree of illumination, although thoughts will continue
to arise although gently, and thinking in the discursive
manner will continue to be active although slowly.
But concentration will be sufficiently strong to detach
him from the world and, as a consequence, to yield
the happiness which accompanies such detachment.
Only those who have attained to this degree can
correctly be regarded as "saved" as only they alone are
unable to fall back into illusion, error, sin, greed, or
sensuality.

In the second degree, there will be more inward
absorption and cerebral processes will entirely fade out.

Freedom from all possibility of anger is a fruit of the
third and higher degree.

(v16, 25:2.97 AND *Perspectives*, P. 347)

ANTHONY: Usually it stays with you unless you do something extraordinarily in opposition to it, and then you may lose it. And sometimes people do have it—for six months, a year, or a certain time—and then it's lost. They have to go back and try again. But generally it tends to stay with you once you get established in it.

If a person makes a persistent effort to reduce the conceptualizing mind to its barest necessity, he will actually at times feel the quietness around him and in him. And he'll see when a thought comes in—even if it tiptoes—it no longer is silent. It's like a big noise coming in. So you begin to recognize that your mind is getting quiet, and you begin to enjoy some of it. It could happen after a couple of days or a couple of weeks, although I may be exaggerating a little bit.

Even if you have it for a little bit, then you have the flavor of what that is. It's very subtle. Your higher Self isn't going to come over and say, "Now you're going to have the quiet mind. Listen." But all of a sudden you're going to say, "Gee, how quiet it is." And then you realize that it's just your mind that has stopped thinking, is quiet; thought is calm. And another nice thing is: thoughts come, and you let them go, too. You don't hold on to them. They come, and they go. For most of us, when thoughts come we say, "Wait a minute!"—and we want to know their history, their genesis, their biography. And we get involved: "All right, next one." And he comes along, and the same thing. And it goes on and on. But with a quiet mind, they come, they go. "Hello, goodbye."

LR: Would you distinguish between the quiet mind and the blank mind?

ANTHONY: The quiet mind is intensely alive. The blank mind is usually very dull. We notice dull minds.

LR: There are PB quotes on meditation that say blankness of mind is really undesirable. In fact it leads to a psychic openness that is very bad. I think it's important to hang on to a notion of awakeness or aliveness. I think it's important to distinguish a dull mind and a quiet mind.

ANTHONY: A quiet mind is also very observant.

LR: Somehow giving up the self-will goes hand in hand in most people's minds with lack of judgement.

ANTHONY: No, as a matter of fact, I would say that you're capable of a fairer judgement. I think you can be, and usually are, much more objective. See, we're not talking about ultimate stages.

A quiet mind, like I said, is very observant. Its observation, very often, is very encompassing, because it observes subtleties that you can't ordinarily see with a mind that's in a state of agitation. And that's what I mean when I say it's intensely alive: not that it's vibrant and dancing about like some lunatic, but it is very observant, very penetrating, and very often it can see subtle truths that the ordinary mind will never be able to grasp or see. They can be communicated to the ordinary mind, but it won't be able to observe them for itself.

LR: So the point is that the still mind is not necessarily contentless.

ANTHONY: Yes. Not necessarily. For example, when you do a sunset meditation, your mind can get very still. You'll go on seeing the sunset, but your mind can get extremely quiet, especially at that moment when the sun pauses and then hovers and then sinks. The contents can still be there.

WHEN THE EGO fails to detain him in formal weaknesses, it will disguise itself anew and direct their strength into subtle and even spiritual channels. If it cannot hold him by his more obvious weaknesses, it will do so by his subtler ones; if not through his shortcomings then through his alleged virtues. It does not find much difficulty with all its craftiness and cunning in perverting his most fervent spiritual aspiration into disguised self-worship and his spiritual experiences into undisguised vanity. Or it will use his sense of remorse, shame, and even humility to point out the futility of his attempts at moral reform and the impossibility of his spiritual aspirations. If he yields to the duplicity and perversity of such moods, he may well abandon the quest in practice and leave it in the air as a matter of theory. But the truth is that this is really a false shame and a false humility.   (v6, 8:4.314)

PD: I think he's also saying you're going to get defeated in a battle, but don't quit the conflict. You're going to lose the battle all the time, but you've got to come back.

ANTHONY: You don't lose unless you quit. As long as you're in there fighting, you're not losing. But if you quit, you lose!

AH: You have to *really* quit.

ANTHONY: If you really quit, you really lose. But even if you *are* losing, if you don't quit, that's all right, because it's going to be like that anyway. The point here is very simple: As long as you do not admit you're defeated, even if you are losing, that's what counts, that you don't admit defeat.

AH: It's a kind of pride that's not egotistical.

ANTHONY: It's not pride; it's endurance. No matter how many times you get knocked down to the canvas—and you will get knocked down enough times—you keep getting up. Even if you take a count to nine, get up. Don't quit.

BS: What precisely do we mean by "the spiritual life?"

ANTHONY: You can get a variety of definitions. The spiritual life is basically an attempt to get back to the wholeness of life, life as a whole, not as a separative thing, to recognize that the life in you is integral, is universal, and not to make the separative ego dominate that or think that it is separate from the rest of life. It's a very subtle thing we're involved in. Like I

said before, when you recognize that your greatest enemy is
the ego, you're on your way.

AN EGO we have, we are; its existence is inescapable if
the cosmic thought is to be activated and the human
evolution in it is to develop. Why has it become, then, a
source of evil, friction, suffering, and horror? The
energy and instinct, the intelligence and desire which
are contained in each individualized fragment of
consciousness, each compounded "I," are not originally
evil in themselves; but when the clinging to them
becomes extreme, selfishness becomes strong. There is a
failure in equilibrium and the gentler virtues are
squeezed out, the understanding that others have rights,
the feeling of goodwill and sympathy, accommodation
for the common welfare—all depart. The natural and
right attention to one's needs becomes enlarged to the
point of tyranny. The ego then exists only to serve itself
at all costs, aggressive to, and exploitive of, all others. It
must be repeated: an ego there must be if there is to be a
World-Idea. But it has to be put, and kept, in its place
(which is not a hardened selfishness). It must adjust to
two things: to the common welfare and to the source of
its own being. Conscience tells him of the first duty,
whether heeded or not; Intuition tells him of the second
one, whether ignored or not. For, overlooked or
misconstrued, the relation between evil and man must
not hide the fact that the energies and intelligence used
for evil derive in the beginning from the divine in man.
They are Godgiven but turned to the service of ungodli-
ness. This is the tragedy, that the powers, talents, and
consciousness of man are spent so often in hatred and
war when they could work harmoniously for the World-
Idea, that his own disharmony brings his own suffering
and involves others. But each wave of development

must take its course, and each ego must submit in the end. He who hardens himself within gross selfishness and rejects his gentler spiritual side becomes his own Satan, tempting himself. Through ambition or greed, through dislike or hate which is instilled in others, he must fall in the end, by the Karma he makes, into destruction by his own negative side.

(v6, 8:1.191 AND *Perspectives*, P. 104)

ANTHONY: Consider this. If consciousness was withdrawn from the body, would a World-Idea appear?

AH: I understood the quote as saying that it would not appear.

ANTHONY: Take consciousness out and there is no appearance, because there is no organism through which an appearance can occur. When you're awake that means that your consciousness is in the body. And through the body as a functioning organism and the senses—concomitant with the functioning of the body—there arises an appearance. The arisal of the appearance is dependent upon the functioning of the organism. If there is no functioning of the organism, there is no appearance. So to that extent we could say that the World-Idea depends upon the individual organism in order for it to get manifested. Otherwise, you're not going to have a World-Idea.

HS: If everything you've got comes from Heaven, any energy, any intelligence, how did you make the mistake?

ANTHONY: Having mandated all these powers to you, this intelligence, this particle of consciousness which has energy—what happened?

HS: I don't want to say it was a primordial, beginningless mistake.

ANTHONY: But why not? Isn't it wrong thinking that leads the person into those errors?

HS: It would be the perpetuation of previous wrongly

held thoughts in the present instant—I would say yes. But to postulate that it never began or that it was beginningless . . .

ANTHONY: Even the Buddha pointed out that as far as he looked he could see no beginning. Why worry about the beginning, anyway? Would you read that part again?

> . . . its existence is inescapable if the cosmic thought is to be activated and the human evolution in it is to develop. Why has it become, then, a source of evil, friction, suffering, and horror? The energy and instinct, the intelligence and desire which are contained in each individualized fragment of consciousness, each compounded "I," are not originally evil in themselves; but when the clinging to them becomes extreme, selfishness becomes strong.

ANTHONY: What happened? These things in themselves are not evil—the energy, the instinct, the intelligence—all these things are included in the compounded "I." What happened? What went wrong? Doesn't he say in the next sentence what went wrong?

SA: Clinging.

ANTHONY: Clinging. Now what does clinging do to it?

NG: That's your mistaken thinking, isn't it?

ANTHONY: Yes. In other words, I had a very pleasant experience two years ago. I cling to it. I'm attached to it. I don't let it go away. I want it *again*. I'm clinging to it. So I repeat it, and I repeat it again. Now the clinging becomes stronger, the selfishness becomes greater. What went wrong originally? It's mistaken thinking.

HS: In the far past, you went off by half an inch and once you're off, you're off. Once your thought is wrong . . .

ANTHONY: Then it has certain consequences.

HS: Every subsequent thought or pattern of thought . . .

ANTHONY: . . . repeats that, makes that stronger. You're off by more and more.

HS: Since you began thinking yourself, it would be safe to assume a lot of mistakes might have slipped in and now there's like a knotted collection of cords where the mistakes are intertwined.

ANTHONY: What would bring about a mistake? Isn't it that you no longer think of the whole, but you're thinking of the part? You're working within the part and you're understanding as a part. Wouldn't that be, again, mistaken thinking? And don't the consequences of that have their own momentum and a snowball effect?

HS: PB speaks about the Ariadne's thread of thought.

ANTHONY: That really is fundamental, isn't it, in his outlook? Thinking is really the fundamental problem. We have to understand the nature of thinking. And the only way we can understand the nature of thinking is by doing precisely what he said and have thinking think about itself. It'll come to a dead stop. But that's beside the point right now.

It's only when a person sees that thinking is creative of his world that he can see that wrong thinking is going to create all the horrors he's going to live with.

HS: You have to do more than begin to think right. You have to go back and unravel previously wrong thought.

ANTHONY: Well, that would be endless. The important thing is to do correct thinking *now*. Never mind about the past. See the thinking that's going on and see how it is mistaken and correct it. Correct thinking is when you're pure observation, pure seeing. As soon as that's deviated from, there's mistaken thinking.

To permit the World-Idea to be manifested through you without you distorting it: that's correct thinking. In other words, if we go to a lower level, we spoke about you being pure looking, pure seeing, pure observation. The perceptual manifold goes on manifesting. You're not interfering. Why? Because you're not going to identify with a portion of that; you're going to remain as mind, unfragmented consciousness. Then that would be correct thinking.

HS: Would you say that a tendency then gets built up, to remain as mind?

ANTHONY: Yes. You remain more and more the whole, and you refuse to identify with the part. This doesn't turn you into some kind of clown, letting people use you for a doormat. As soon as you identify with a portion, with that mind which divided itself into a subject and an object, as soon as you permit that, then the consequences are inevitable. They must follow.

CDA: So even if you saw that you had all of these vices or weaknesses, to try to correct them within the frame of the ego subject . . .

ANTHONY: Well, we have to try to do that anyway, but the trouble is that your ego will get reinforced. That is not the way to ultimate success. But that it will not guarantee ultimate success does not preclude the efforts that you should make to overcome that. Ultimate success will only come when you reinstate yourself in the original and undivided whole that you are.

FD: If we say consciousness clings to these thoughts and consequently mistaken thinking takes place, then that implies that the mistake was inherent in the consciousness to begin with, and the origin of the problem is still within the higher Self, is still within consciousness.

ANTHONY: You're looking for an escape route. You're going to get into the etiology or the genesis of the disease instead of getting rid of the disease. You say: "Now all this is due to the fact that my consciousness is fallen, etc., etc." And I'm saying never mind that. What counts now is: Look, and keep looking; understand the way your mind operates, see what it's doing, trace it back, and you'll see that eventually your mind or your consciousness is splitting up. Watch that process until the point where you get immersed in it and you become just pure seeing.

Before you get that doctor to pull this arrow out of your chest, you want to know what his name is, his vocation, where his family comes from, and you go down the list. And by the time I finish telling you all that, you'll be dead and buried.

FD: But practicality has to be somewhat connected with theory.

ANTHONY: But don't you see? I try to restrict myself to the immediacy of the quote that's involved and I keep trying to cut off these questions that will take us to an exposition of the whole doctrine. Then you're going to ask me, "Why did consciousness cling to something? What's inherent in consciousness?" Then we have to go back and try to understand how the Idea of Man in its full development is included in Being and how it is all non-evolutionary. I don't want to go into that.

All I want to do is present you with the immediacy of the quotation, the extreme value it has if you just restrict your understanding to what we're talking about. The tendency to become theoretical is rampant.

The mind is always providing its own escape route. Very often we think that the questions we ask are relevant, and I have to go along with that because I don't want you to get too angry with me. But the fact is that here most of those questions are really irrelevant. We're getting down to a level of understanding that has to be applied to the immediacy of the situation.

When I speak about ferreting out the source of the ego, I'm not speaking about theory; I'm speaking about something you've got to do. You've got to watch every time a thought comes into your mind. You've got to understand the nature of that thought; you've got to see what it's doing. You've got to trace it to its origin. You've got to keep doing that with the perceptual field, from moment to moment, as it's going on. You can't allow yourself to be comfortable in the psyche. It's what I call "the living dead."

And we're all guilty of it. It's very hard work to constantly keep looking at your mind, seeing the way the ego is always surreptitiously or nefariously, slyly, throwing those things up, always without letting go, never stopping.

NG: Suppose you see that, what's the next thing?

ANTHONY: After the shock wears off, if you see, then you begin to get an idea of the task that's ahead. You get an idea of the magnitude of the task ahead of you, because you've penetrated this teaching to some extent now, and you're going to have to start applying some of it. That's the hurtful part. When you see it, you'll have no need of anyone.

NG: Is it that clear?

ANTHONY: You *know*. I don't mean by that you'll know the Ultimate. I mean you know what your task is. I'm really trying to get down on the ground now. That's why, more and more often, I'm going to restrict conversation. Not that I don't want you to talk, but every now and then I just want to corner your attention on a point that is of *extreme* value.

THE EGO is a collection of thoughts circulating around a fixed but empty centre. If the habits of many, many reincarnations had not given them such strength and persistence, they could be voided. The reality —
MIND— could then reveal Itself. (v6, 8:2.37)

ANTHONY: Watch the constant metamorphosing of thought that's going on in your mind. It tends to have a certain structure, it tends to repeat itself. But what it's talking about, and what it's constantly repeating—there's nothing there. If you stop, put out the lights, and just let the first thought come into your mind and let it go—you'll see what it's referring to—there's nothing there. The thought itself is empty; there's nothing to it, it's insubstantial, it's a phantasmagoria. If anything shows up the nullity of our existence, it's when we engage in that kind of activity all the time.

It's the first part of the quote that has to be understood in all its force—that this gossamer thread of thought is constantly metamorphosing itself from instant to instant about nothing, about nothing. Yet, because of its structure, its dynamics, around something which, as we said, is insubstantial, we are chained to it. The rest of the quote is quite secondary if you understand this.

FDS: So if I search in my meditations for this fixed center that I sense or feel, I won't be able to find it.

ANTHONY: There isn't any. We speak about thought, fantasizing or metamorphosing, changing from instant to instant. What's the center around which it is doing that? Is there some pole there that it wraps itself around? Or is it its insubstantiality, its lack of a center? The most direct way to understand it is just to go over in your mind what you do all the time, how you're preoccupied with nullity. But because that preoccupation is repetitive, you think there's some reality to it. You know, like if you say something enough times, you'll believe it.

Remember the analogy we used? There's a tree standing by the bank of a river, and it is reflected in the river. The river is traversing, it's moving on, and the tree is reflected in the river. That constant and incessant changing of the water in the image of the tree would be like the continuity of thought which we call the ego. But when you say it has a common center, an empty center, it would be the same as imagining that this river is flowing all the time: The image reflected in the river doesn't have what you might call constant being, but the being of the image is being incessantly changed from moment to moment. That would be like the ego. It has a form: the image of the tree in the river. It has this form, but that which constitutes it is incessantly being changed from instant to instant. So there's nothing *there* at any one time. You no sooner say, "That's it," than the water has moved on and other particles have taken its place. And this is always going on.

The ego is also something like that. There are always thoughts, thoughts which are preoccupied with themselves, but they never stand still long enough to be able to say they are.

Just watch your mind, watch the way it repeats itself, how thought after thought changes from one thought to another, right in front of your very eyes, and this tends to be repetitive and tends to have a certain power, and you think it's *about* something. You have a thought, and you think it's about some *thing*. And it's not. It isn't about anything.

AH: Is the thought mine? Does it belong to me?

ANTHONY: That's the very thing that's depriving you of finding out who this "I" is, because you're preoccupied with what is *not* "I." You're preoccupied with this process that's always going on.

You mean it never occurs to you when a thought is going on in your mind to strike it out, smash it, destroy it, and say, "You! You are an S.O.B! You deprive me of my peace of mind!" Doesn't it occur to you? No, huh?

THERE IS no real ego but only a quick succession of thoughts which constitutes the "I" process. There is no separate entity forming the personal consciousness but only a series of impressions, ideas, images revolving around a common centre. The latter is completely empty; the feeling of something being there derives from a totally different plane—that of the Overself.

(v6, 8:2.31)

NG: Suppose someone can recognize that process to some degree. Is PB saying that when you reach that emptiness, you then have a feeling that there *is* something there despite the emptiness? Or is he saying that you recognize that your daily thoughts are really about nothing, and still you have, in that daily life, the feeling that there *is* really someone or something and that feeling comes from the plane of the Overself?

ANTHONY: I think you said the right thing. When you investigate, when you're looking at your thoughts, you analyze and you see there's nothing there. You understand the illusory nature. You understand that fundamentally the ego is of an illusory nature. There's no reality there. But nonetheless there is the experience that you are real, that there's something real. And there you could, of course, distinguish between two things. On the one hand, existence, and on the other, the fundamentally "illusory" nature of the ego.

In the depths of your heart you know that you *really are.* But when you look out at the world around you, when you look into your mind and watch these thoughts come and go, and they try to present you with some kind of panorama or view, you can see that it's all false. But the feeling that there is some reality is coming from the depths of your heart. That is real.

NG: You're not speaking about a special meditation?

ANTHONY: No, I'm speaking about the most ordinary thing possible—that every time you look into your mind and you watch your thoughts changing, one after the other, and you persist in looking at this, after a while you begin to see that you're identifying with something that's absolutely illusory, that has no existence, that practically is and isn't at the same time.

To be preoccupied with that is to reduce yourself to this illusory kind of being, whereas if you stay removed from that, if you keep that at a distance or, better still, if you don't permit it—then you feel something quite different. Fundamentally, you would be feeling something coming from your own reality, the reality that you really are.

But the fact that this is not understood shows you are not really introspecting into yourself. You're not looking at the thoughts that the mind is constantly throwing up at you and making you subservient to. You've got to see that. That's the most important thing about these quotes.

> THE TEACHING that the ego does not exist—repeated so often in so parrot-like a way—can help no one, can only create intellectual confusion and thus harm the search for truth. But the teaching that the ego is only an idea—however strongly held by the mind—and as such does exist, can help everyone in the struggle for self-mastery and can throw intellectual light on the search for truth.
>
> (v6, 8:2.27)

> THE EGO is nothing more than a shadow. Its stuff and reality are merely that transient ever-changing play of light and colour. It exists—a word whose very meaning, "to be placed outside," is also metaphysically true. For he who immerses himself in its consciousness places himself outside the consciousness of Overself.
>
> (v6, 8:2.29)

AP: Let's discuss what is the ego consciousness that immerses itself in the thought stream.

ANTHONY: That *is* the ego consciousness. If you're immersed in the thought stream, you're in the ego's consciousness. If you're not immersed in it, then you're in the Overself's consciousness. I'm trying to speak in a practical way. I'm saying something like this: If you pay attention to your thoughts, you're in the ego; ignore them, you're out of it.

See how subtle it is? Very, very subtle. Just a shift in attention and emphasis—if the attention shifts into the thought, identifies with the thought, you're in the ego consciousness. Shift the attention out of the ego consciousness, don't identify with the ego, the thoughts, and you'll be with the Overself. But I know you won't try it. You won't believe me.

RS: I believe it and I understand it.

ANTHONY: Do it! [*laughter*]

RS: But I think unless we can get rid of the thoughts, we are not in that consciousness.

ANTHONY: Tomorrow morning I've got to go to the dentist and get a tooth pulled out, and so all night I'm thinking about the dentist—all night. I spend eight hours worrying about it. I'm living in the ego consciousness; whereas if I push that thought aside and don't go into it, don't identify with it, then I won't be living in the ego consciousness, I won't be suffering anxiety, I won't be in pain. But every time I lapse, every time I think, "Ah! The dentist tomorrow," boom! I'm in pain. "Get out, get out quick, hurry up, get out of the ego . . . Oh! I feel better."

RS: The thoughts might be away from the dentist and still there might be some other thoughts.

ANTHONY: Oh, no, no, no! It's an *analogy*. The whole idea is if you get out of the thought of the ego, don't get into another one. Stay out of thought! Stay out of it.

Remember how we spoke about it? You show your faith in the higher when you reject the thoughts that the ego is proffering you to identify with. Every time you push away the thought and you refuse to identify with it, you're showing your faith in the higher power.

AH: Anthony, is there a way, in thought, to show faith in the higher power? What if I have very spiritual thoughts? Very sublime, metaphysical . . . [*laughter*]

ANTHONY: You notice the way already a pride and greed are coming in? "I've got very spiritual thoughts. I've got to be better than everybody else. There's no doubt in my mind about it."

AH: Spiritual seems to mean not having any thoughts; the best ones are not ones at all.

ANTHONY: The best ones are the ones you refuse to identify with. Then you will know something about spirituality, because it will actually be happening.

KD: If I'm paying attention, if I'm listening to the quote and I'm not being distracted by thoughts, I'm certainly not in the state of the Overself consciousness.

ANTHONY: Tell me, if you listen very intently and you understand what I'm saying, who is it that understands? Whose power is it?

KD: Well, you're talking about the understanding, obviously not the ego.

ANTHONY: We're speaking here quietly, we're making some remarks, and you're listening. And of course it's obvious that you have to listen to the thoughts I'm expressing, and you're not in the Overself consciousness, sure. But then you suddenly understand what I'm saying. To whom does that power to understand belong? To the ego? For instance, when we understand the illusory nature of the ego, do you think it's the ego that understands that? So that power by which you understand is the divine within you.

KD: If your attention isn't being distracted and absorbed by this repetitive thinking process, then there can be some kind of contact with the World-Idea, with the wisdom that's unfolding.

ANTHONY: There would be a much more spontaneous operation of the intelligence, which is, like we said, the divinity within us. You make it personal by intruding with your reactions and preventing it from operating. That's why I point out: If you have faith in the higher, you do not pay attention to the stream of thoughts that is constantly transforming itself from one into another, the senselessness that goes on and on *ad nauseam*. You just reject all that, and you keep your mind still.

I'm not saying that every other moment you're going to be inspired with illuminating thoughts that will remake the world. I'm not saying that. But there will occur to you moments where the intelligence will spontaneously respond to whatever the situation calls for. That spontaneity of intelligence is the divinity within you, and right then and there you'll be experiencing that higher power within you. You don't have to have a world-devastating illumination and the light of a million suns shining to be in the Overself. It's so close, but we fail to recognize it all the time. That's our problem.

KD: When I first heard you talk about that shift in attention—that if you get rid of thoughts then you can experience this Overself consciousness—at first I thought that my normal thinking would be replaced by some light or some great thing, but that's putting in another thought.

ANTHONY: That's another thought you have, sure. It's always ducking the issue, so to speak.

KD: So what you're describing, why it's so difficult is. . .

ANTHONY: It's not difficult.

KD: . . . is because the Overself is not going to be another object of my thinking, another content.

ANTHONY: Yes. Another point we made was the need to understand the depth of penetration, the way the dragon penetrates through all of these things so that it entices us. So if you have a thought, if you have an image in your mind, you could experience the fascination and glamour with which the dragon is trying to suck you into the thought. All you have to do is have an image: You're cooked.

CDA: Is that glamour or fascination part of the very nature of thought? Is it just a tool the ego uses, that fascination?

ANTHONY: That would certainly be part of it, that it's

used by the ego. But why do you have difficulty understanding that it's the very nature of imagery to bind us to it?

CDA: Is that because we've created it ourselves?

ANTHONY: Yes, we've created it. It's also our past, and the past is always something that we look back to with nostalgia.

HS: Anthony, you say as we sit here and we talk, "Don't identify with the thoughts as they arise and you are the Overself consciousness." You say if we understand it, the understanding that you're talking about would be like that non-identification with the arisal of the thought?

ANTHONY: I think maybe we'd better put this in the proper context. Let's say you're just by yourself sitting down and you allow thoughts to occur, one after the other, and you identify with these thoughts, and you experience them to the extent that you can. To that extent that you have identified with the lesser, with the ego consciousness, there's nothing you're going to know. You're not going to find out anything, because the thoughts are always about the past, the known, what has happened. They're not going to tell you anything, because they've got nothing to offer. But they will go on and on and on. And I repeat this: The identification with that is to believe in the ego, to live in the ego consciousness until you get nauseous.

Now, the other thing I was trying to explain was in a different context: how you can see that you can live in the Overself consciousness. We're talking, we're having a discussion, and in the discussion, let's say, some very subtle points are being made. In the process of following very attentively the points that are being made there's a kind of discussion in *jnana* [knowledge] taking place. There may come a point where you understand something, and at the same time you'll experience a certain happiness, a quiet happiness. And I'm pointing to that and saying that's the divinity within you that understands these things, not the ego. The ego doesn't understand these things, but the divinity within you understands these things.

Now obviously when I speak about the divinity within you, it would be like what we refer to as the soul within the person. It's the soul inside that understands these things. And you can temporarily or briefly experience living in the Overself's consciousness.

Don't think that the Overself consciousness must be some extra rapture and ecstasy, where you swoon because you're so ecstatic; it doesn't have to be that way. The Overself consciousness could be very peaceful and very quiet. You could experience the nobility of its peace and the certitude of its understanding. It could be that way, too. And it would be experienced in a discussion taking place about some very subtle point.

HS: If it is a discussion that's taking place about a subtle point, and the point is made that the Overself consciousness is experienceable in terms of its certitude . . .

ANTHONY: And understanding—wouldn't that be like being in the Overself's consciousness?

HS: Just to understand it, right here?

ANTHONY: Isn't that why you stopped to ask again? Because you doubt that that is it—that understanding of these things. You say, "But can it be such a trivial thing?" It's not trivial. Rather, it's because we're so gross that we see it as so ethereal and so trivial. If we were capable of purifying ourselves to some extent, then that trivial point that we're talking about could become quite important. But I think you got the point: It's the Overself within, the soul within, that understands.

NG: And that's why you get so happy. Thoughts never make you happy; they never keep their promises.

ANTHONY: They never do; that's right.

SO LONG as we persist in taking the ego at its own
valuation as the real Self, so long are we incapable of
discovering the truth about the mind or of penetrating
to its mysterious depths. It is a pretender, but so long as
no enquiry is instituted it goes on enjoying the status of
the real Self. Once an enquiry into its true nature is
begun in the proper manner and continued as long as
necessary, this identification with ego may subside and
surrender to the higher.   (v6, 8:4.386)

KD: It's interesting that he stresses enquiry and not meditation. He doesn't say go meditate and stop all thinking. I think
that this point of enquiry implies more of a philosophic enquiry,
penetration, an attempt to understand rather than . . .

ANTHONY: Rather than not thinking.

KD: Right. You always say observation is looking. I think
that might be included in what he meant about enquiry.

ANTHONY: Yes, the ego will always pretend that it is the reality, and if it is not challenged, it will go on doing so. Even
when it's challenged, the challenge has to be based on an understanding of how to undermine the ego and what criteria
you'll use.

The way it's presented when we read about it, the ego
affirms that it is the reality. Most of us think we could push
it aside and say, "You're not real." But at the slightest incon-
venience—like if you're walking across the street and a car
comes by, you'll jump; the totality of your being will be involved in making a leap of about twenty-eight feet. Or someone calls you a name and the totality of your ego comes up
and defends itself. We have to think of the ego under these
circumstances.

We're not to think, "He's a nice fellow, the ego. I meet him every day; we come here; we sit down and have a cup of coffee. He's a real nice fellow." That's not the ego. The ego is the guy that, when you really say, "I don't believe you," he says, "Oh, no? We'll find out!" And so, if there's any unpleasant news, you'll see a gut reaction turn you inside out; you'll faint or swoon—that's the ego I'm talking about. That's the guy who's got it all. He's the one who says, "I'm real." Not the guy that you meet when you drink your coffee. That's not the guy. It's this guy here who says, "I'm real, and you're going to kowtow."

TS: What does he mean by "an enquiry begun in the proper manner"?

ANTHONY: I would think that it means the use of your critical faculties, your rational understanding. In the first three chapters of *The Quest of the Overself*, PB goes through a very rational analysis of the ego, and the net result of that analysis is that you're not the ego. You remember that, right? He goes to the point where he points out that we are not even our perceptions. He goes through a very careful analysis in those chapters. I would say that's one of the ways you could start off an enquiry into the nature of the ego, a way which is rational and firmly based on the reasoning processes.

DB: What is it, precisely, that has an interest in resisting these reactions and responses and thought processes?

ANTHONY: This question always comes up in one form or another. Remember when Plotinus answers the question, "Who is it that wants to do this?" He points out that it depends upon which phase of the soul is dominant. Is it that phase of the soul which is completely immersed in the ego and dominated by the ego which wants to have an understanding of the ego? Or is it that phase of the soul which is engaged in critical understanding and trying to understand the world around it—in other words, the reasoning phase of the soul? Is it that phase of the soul which wants to know?

Any time we speak about these things, we must keep in mind the context. If we say there's a part of the consciousness or if, in looking into ourselves, we identify ourselves with the images which are thrown across the screen and we say, "Well, that's who I am," then you're speaking about the soul as *that*. If you're speaking about the person who is looking at the images that are spun out across the screen and who reasons about them and tries to find a way to understand what is going on, then you could say, "*That's* the soul," and not the fellow who's identified with the images. And if you can go further and say that there's a part of you that brings about the cessation of thought, by having thought preoccupied with itself, then you could say, "*That's* the soul." Let's try to keep in mind that we're talking only in terms of the context of what the soul is identified with.

DB: So would you say that this self-enquiry takes place within the rational part of the soul?

ANTHONY: Well, who do you think would ask such a question, "Why this endless, stupid suffering?" Do you think it's going to be the animal?

DB: No. It's the rational soul as identified with the animal for whom this is a problem.

ANTHONY: So when we speak about the soul, we could speak about a portion of it which is completely irrational, immersed in the body; we could speak about a portion of it which is rational and thinks about these things; we could think of a portion of it which is absolutely intellectual.[4] And so the question always has to be asked with that in the background. So who is it that is sick and tired of being transfixed, transposed, or nailed to the cross of suffering? Is it the stupid animal, Brother Ass?

DB: No.

ANTHONY: You got the point then.

KD: What is it about enquiry that has the power to divest

this ego of that fundamental anxiety that it operates with—
that total reactive tendency? It can't be the conceptual understanding we operate with.

ANTHONY: Well, yes, it would be more than conceptual.
But I think the question you're asking is more like this: What
is there in the power of Truth that releases you from ignorance? If we take a lesser example: You see the sun rise, and
you go around for a couple of hundred thousand lives believing the sun rises. Now by that time it should be a thoroughly
ingrained habit, with no possibility of its ever being dislodged.
But somehow you reach a certain point of understanding—
someone explains to you what is really happening—and now
you understand that it isn't the sun that rises. It seems that
there's a power in reason that disabuses you from illusion.

KD: What is that?

ANTHONY: [softly] What is that power that Truth has? I
can't tell you that.

KD: But it sounds like whatever this mysterious enquiry
is, that has to do with what we call *jnana.*

ANTHONY: Yes, to understand the nature of the ego and
everything that's related to it.

KD: Is it because enquiry uses the very thing, thought,
that has created this problem, this wrong habit?

ANTHONY: I thought your question was much more
fundamental and that is: What is the power that Truth has
that compels us to believe in it?

TS: As you said earlier, the understanding that occurs
when thought is still is that presence of the Overself, and it is
the act of the Overself. And isn't it that understanding as a
rational act of the soul, that is the power of Truth?

ANTHONY: I thought she [KD] was asking a very fundamental question which I get scared of, too, sometimes. That is,
the world appears; and I start analyzing that appearance. And
in a short while I'm reduced to a state of absolute uncertainty.

I don't know what is really out there any more. If I go through a systematic analysis of experience, and I analyze the world that appears, I begin to recognize that it is *not* what it appears to be. And I thought that her question is: What is this strange power? What is it? What is this strange power of understanding, when a person understands something? I don't know.

But, maybe we could speak to the last part of the quote. That I think is available to us—where PB says that once that power to identify with the lower is released from that process, then it can be offered up to the higher. I prefer that you look at this in a practical way.

You're looking, you're observing your mind, and you notice that there's a tendency on the part of the mind or some part of you to always identify with the images that are taking place. You notice it after a while; it doesn't take much. But you begin to see: Any image arises, there's a part of you that immediately identifies with it. "I'm going to be a great composer, great writer," boom! I'm identified with that thought. "What should I make for dinner tonight?" It doesn't matter because I'm not eating, nor is anyone else, but the thoughts go on, and you keep identifying. [*laughter*]

That power to identify with the various thoughts—if it is freed from that tendency to identify with any of the images that occur, now what happens? And I think he says now it must be offered to the higher; it must be surrendered to the higher. If we think about it practically, then that means that instead of looking at the images which are going on all the time in my mind, I ignore them but lie in a state of quiescence. What will that attention do if it's not going to identify with the images? He says "surrender it to the higher," but what does that mean?

HS: The attention remains in its self, its source?

ANTHONY: Yes. It remains self-absorbed. That's a practical way of understanding what that surrender means. Now we're speaking about work that must be *done* on oneself, and this has to be done as often as possible, at any opportunity or moment that circumstance or time permits.

AH: Is this to suggest that the very practical meaning of this is that the ego can only surrender by getting out of the way?

ANTHONY: You see the difficulty of speaking in such absolute terms. We spoke about the fact that there are images, and I can identify with these images, and to the extent that I identify with these images, I'm living in the ego-consciousness. Now, to the extent that I disidentify with the images, try *not* to live in the ego-consciousness, I get closer to the Source, to my *own* consciousness, which is more than the ego-consciousness.

The point we have to make here is: If we try to *describe* these things, instead of having these absolute categories like "ego," then I can deal with my problems; I can communicate and talk to you. To think of it as a fixed entity is very harmful; but if you think of it in this contextual way, what the word "ego" means according to the way I'm using it, it is not a thing that is fixed. As soon as you start using it in a reified way, I'm in trouble, and so are you.

So we will go back to the practical thing that we're talking about. I'm looking at my own mind, and I'm watching all the thoughts. They're always trying to draw me in: "Come here, come here! I want your attention, kid. I want you to be preoccupied with me all the time. Me, me, me, me, me." That's all the ego.

I keep fighting that tendency. It's the ego fighting its own tendency! You say paradox, the thief set out to catch a thief. I don't like those kinds of words, because the truth of the matter is that I am interested in my own evolution. This little ego here, stupid as it is, wants to evolve and become a little better. So it has to fight and struggle with its own tendencies to become a little better.

To say, "Well, the ego won't succeed"—is just plain

wrong. It will succeed; given enough time and raw circumstances, it'll succeed. It will *not* succeed in crucifying itself and destroying itself; we know that. But the long evolutionary development is its business—of course in conjunction with the World-Idea—but it is its business. So the *ego* has to do these things. Nobody out there is going to come here and do it for me. So let's stick to this paradoxical nature of the reality we're confronted with so that we can deal with it.

So, these images are in my mind. The attention wants to go and identify with them. I resist it. When I say "I" I'm talking about *this* ego resisting that. "No, I'm not going to do it." "Oh, come on. Look at how lovely I am!" "No! I won't!" So you fight it. You keep pushing it away. Eventually, little by little, you do begin to resist this enticement that thoughts are always exercising. It is you—you as the ego—that has succeeded somewhat. Little by little you get to a point where you can disidentify with the process and say, "No, I'm not going to look. I'm going to keep the attention absorbed, wrapped up in itself, self-attentive." Then when I do this, I'm liable to reach a higher understanding.

If we describe it like this, if we keep in the realm of the practical, in the everyday activities of your thinking, you'll be dealing with metaphysics in this really very practical way. At least as far as I'm concerned, it will give me some indication that you *do* understand metaphysics in a practical way. Because when you read about metaphysics and then you talk about it in a class, that's fine. But then when you start talking about the way you're working it out, applying it on yourself, it's a whole different ball game. In the very description of the work that you put yourself through, there will be a revelation, or at least an illustration, of how much you understand of these teachings—by actually looking at the fantasies, by saying, "I'm not going to identify with them," by bringing this metaphysical work right down home.

So LONG as the ego's rule is preserved, so long will the karmic tendencies which come with it be preserved. But when its rule is weakened they too will automatically be starved and weakened. To start this process, start trying to take an impersonal detached view. (v6, 8:3.84)

ANTHONY: All he's saying is that the way to start weakening these karmic tendencies is to be impersonal, to develop an impersonal consciousness. Analyze them, and continue to do so. The understanding in itself is basically impersonal, and it helps you get detached from them. Not overnight, but gradually. You have to keep analyzing your habits from the point of view of the impersonal consciousness, so that you can weaken them. That's the same as when you stop eating and you starve yourself. There's a weakening of these habitual tendencies. It acts in a similar way when a person analyzes and tries to understand the nature of his cravings and objectify them. That very process of understanding and objectifying the nature of his cravings, that process of objectification, brings about disidentification with them.

HE: Does this go hand in hand with the exercise of the will to reject the thoughts?

ANTHONY: I think of it not so much as an act of the will; I think of it as an act of seeing, knowing. If I start saying, "I'm going to will this," then I start getting greedy. The ego comes into play; effort is going to be made. I want to be bet ter than the other guy. Whereas if I just try to observe very clearly, "This is what's going on," then the consequences will be that the intelligence within will spontaneously operate on that. You first have to see what is really happening before the true, spontaneous intelligence can operate on it. But we don't see what's truly happening. We see what we *think* is happening, which is a whole different ball game.

HE: What we spoke about before as watching, observing

and not identifying—is that an exercise that you have to begin in meditation or while not going about your daily business?

ANTHONY: Do it every time the thought arises. Every time the thought arises, try to experience this witnessing or this impersonality of consciousness. Try to observe, try to see. But there's no one there that sees anything, because as soon as you say there's someone there, you're no longer seeing. You're like in a corner of the room or in the balcony somewhere. But if you speak about just seeing, there's no one there. There's only that which is seen, which will include who's seeing and what he or she is seeing. And the best way is to try to do it every time you think of it. Pure observation, pure looking, pure seeing.

■ ■ ■

ANTHONY: PB points out that there's a need to engage in the quest, which consists of intense concentration, meditation, reflection, and discipline or purification.

THE ASPIRANT will receive personal knowledge from within, as apart from mere teaching from without, only to the extent that he has inwardly prepared himself to receive it. The fruits of the quest cannot be separated from the disciplines of the quest. He is considered capable of grasping philosophic truth when, either now or in a previous existence, he has to some degree purified his understanding by self-discipline, introverted it by meditation, and tranquillized it by reflection. When his mind has habituated itself to this kind of keen, abstract thinking and in some measure has developed the capacity to rest absorbed in its own tranquil centre, when the emotions have purified themselves of personal and animal taints, he has prepared himself for the highest kind of knowledge.

For then he is able to use this highly concentrated, well purified, efficiently serene consciousness as an instrument with which to engage himself in a quest to understand in true perspective what the ego really is and to look deep into the nature of the mind itself. For then his self-examination will be free from the emotional distortions, the materialistic impediments of the unpurified, unstilled, and unconcentrated consciousness. The truth about his own existence and the world's existence can then be seen as never before.   (v3, 2:9.1)

ANTHONY: Remember when the Dalai Lama was here? He gave us three books. What do the three books stand for? The *Tripitaka*, the three canons, the three baskets. What are the three baskets? One is called the law or the discipline, the *vinaya* rules; the second one, meditation; and the third, understanding.

Well, what are the three things he just told you? Discipline, meditation, reflection. And what does the Vedantist say you have to do? Self-purificational discipline, concentrational meditation, and reflection. Those are the three things that you have to do. You will not get it any other way. You think somebody's going to come and whisper in your ear, right?

These three have to be employed and it isn't going to get you to *nirvana* overnight. It's going to get you acquainted with what and who you are. Then you worry about getting to *nirvana*. But if this ego is the obstacle, then you should get to know about that first. But you're not going to transcend or transgress its boundaries.

THE DEGREE of ego-attachment which you will find at the centre of a man's consciousness is a fairly reliable index to the degree of his spiritual evolution.

(v6, 8:4.452)

ANTHONY: In other words, how attached a man is to his ego is an index to his spiritual growth.

RC: But that doesn't mean we should fill out report cards.

ANTHONY: I think you should. Everybody at night should go over his report card.

EC: To really be honest with oneself is very difficult.

ANTHONY: That's why one has to practice constantly. The Pythagorean recall exercise is a good idea, in which you review at night what you did all day long. In almost all the schools, especially the ancient schools, the *one* requirement, the one exercise that everybody was given was: Before you go to sleep at night, try reviewing everything you did during the day. Reflect on what you did, try to understand what you did, try to understand the ideas or the values that you were implementing. If you don't, your day is wasted. You got no benefit out of it. Try again tomorrow. And *nobody* in class believed this. You'll be aghast in the beginning at some of what you did, but after a while you learn not to do it, little by little. Little by little a certain impartiality is gained.

Then you employ the other exercise where you try to visualize and imagine yourself as you should act. Employ the two simultaneously if you expect a little detachment from the ego.[5]

But basically, you could see what he's saying there. I don't think we have a ruler but each one can decide for himself how strong his attachment is to his ego. So if someone calls you an S.O.B. and you kick him in the shins before the words are finished, you have a relative idea of how strong your attachment is. On the other hand, if you just ignore it and walk away and don't even react, that gives you a different scale. Your report card is different.

RC: This quote seems to bring in the idea of how strongly I am attached to the succession of thoughts.

ANTHONY: Yes. So, in this succession of thoughts, if a thought comes up you can get on it as though you were a horseback rider and it takes you away. And then there's a case where a person, before he jumps on the thought, thinks about it and pauses and then jumps on the horse and goes away. And there's another instance where you pause and then you say, "No I'm not going to jump on it," and you let the thought go away. There are three different degrees right there of how attached you are to your ego, if, as we said, the ego is a succession of thoughts which are actualizing themselves from instant to instant.

> IT IS EASY to recognize some of the attachments from which he must loose himself—the greeds, the lusts, and the gluttonies—but it is not so easy to recognize the subtler ones. These start with attachment to his own ideas, his own beliefs; they end with attachment to his own ego. (v6, 8:4.380)

ANTHONY: That's one of the reasons I spent a lot of time on astrology. The only way you're going to see what your attachments and your beliefs are is when you get to know your degrees. Until then you don't know what your attachments and beliefs are. But when you isolate these things you can take, let's say, the functioning of a planet in your chart, on a certain degree, and see that *this is the way you are*. I don't care what you tell me. This is the way you are. This is the way you're going to be. This is the way you're going to act.[6]

PB's not saying "Get rid of it." You can't. Because as long as you have to express yourself in the world—and there's nothing wrong with expressing yourself in the world—this is the way you're going to express yourself. The stupidity is not to understand that this idea that you're working through to express yourself is an *idea*. It's not *you*. Don't get attached to it. Look at it impersonally. Try to understand the way you operate—functionally, impersonally. And after a while you'll see this is that next step—until you understand this, to talk about renouncing the ego is absurd. Because you're going to see the way these things work *in* you, the way they're going to trick you and say, "Oh, sure, now we'll move on and renounce the ego." [*laughter*] You see? They're very quick.

You really can make a marvelous use of astrology and especially the degree symbolism to understand the particular beliefs and ideas that you are attached to. I wouldn't use the word "attached," I'd say you are "*mis-identified with.*" If you take one of those ways of working that you identify with, one of those degrees, and you understand the meaning so that it is open and available to you, then you can objectively see that this is the way you operate. You can learn to be impersonal about your ego and to watch that happen. So it's really worthwhile. That was one of the great values of astrology as far as I was able to see.

HE: Would you say that if you got to see it impersonally you would be able to operate with a more positive aspect of the degree?

ANTHONY: Yes, more efficiently. But don't expect it the first time.

IT IS LESS EASY to see and even more necessary to
understand that this ego, this subject, is itself an object
to a higher part of the mind.   (v6, 8:2.67)

RG: If the ego is looking at the ego, it could never see itself objectively. Whereas if the ego is an object to a higher mind, then by making the ego an object of its enquiry, the higher mind would also be imposing the discipline. It has to be something other than the ego that looks.

ANTHONY: You can call that higher mind the reasoning soul, and the reasoning soul is what brings manifestation about. The soul, through the intermediary phase, the reason-

ing phase, manifests itself as the ego. The ego is a manifestation of that. And each and every soul has, within itself, the
matter through which it can manifest itself.

Now, this matter, through which it can manifest itself, is
not chemical atoms. Think of this matter as retaining the tendencies, the potencies which are a continuous drift of the
way manifestation has been going on. If we think of that as
the ego, and don't confuse it with the reasoning soul or with
the Overself's consciousness, then we always have to locate
ourselves in that ego, in that matrix of possibilities. We always
have to take our stand there to be realistic about what's
going on.

So if you say, "Well, I wanted to become a spiritual
quester," many people would say there was a call from the
soul. Sure, I think that's very feasible and it happens very
often when there's some call from within the soul, a noticed
sound, that then the ego reverts and turns back. But in general, the way we're speaking now, we have to think of this
ego as all these tendencies, and it is up to us to generate those
tendencies that are conducive towards an expansive enlarged
version of the ego so that it includes within itself greater
and greater comprehension. It is the ego that ultimately and
finally, paradoxical as it may sound, gets enlightened.

HS: Can the knowledge of the ego as a matrix of possibilities, and not as some self-inherently existent "I," be assimi-
lated?

ANTHONY: Sure. It might take a little time to get it, but
you'll assimilate it. You'll be able to watch vigilantly and see it
operate in front of your very clean mental eyes.

HS: And you're not talking about conception now?

ANTHONY: No, I'm not talking about conception. I'm
talking about you actually seeing with your mental eyes. You
see someone praise you and you feel good, and someone criticize you and you scream. And you can see the ego's wings

flapping as clearly as you can feel the pole you bump into.

DD: Can one aspect of the ego, which is more conscious, more learned, observe other voices in the ego?

ANTHONY: No. What PB is speaking about in this quote is the Witness I. It's different. For instance, you wake up from a dream and you see that you don't need the dream ego to operate. So you could wake up from egoistic consciousness and see that you're the Witness I and that you don't need the ego consciousness to work with. That requires explanation all by itself, just like in the quotes where he goes through the fact that the ego is part of the World-Idea and therefore cannot be destroyed.

To take the Witness position means that you already know what the ego is. You've stepped out of it once you're in the Witness position. PB recommends certain exercises where he tells you to try to take the Witness position, because all you need is *one* glimpse in order to step out of the ego and to see it for what it is. Then when it takes you, you know.

RG: But it isn't the ego that takes the Witness position. The ego is seen from the Witness position.

ANTHONY: The ego cannot take the Witness position. But remember, it will always try to infiltrate. You know, just like the Fifth Column during the war?

DB: Ultimately it sounds like the association with thought has to be broken, that that is the real distinction.

ANTHONY: The real distinction is that you do have to step outside of your thoughts, once. Otherwise you'll never get to the core of what ego is.

RG: I thought there was a middle level in there which was neither the Overself consciousness nor the ego, but the rational. We read: "For then he is able to use this highly concentrated, well purified, efficiently serene consciousness as an instrument with which to engage himself in a quest to understand in true perspective what the ego really is." Now what is that serene consciousness? It doesn't seem to be the ego the way we've been talking about it, and it doesn't seem to be the Overself.

ANTHONY: Again you are making classifications that are very rigid. Given this situation where you put yourself through this discipline and meditation and all that, then the infiltration of the higher Witness consciousness can operate in you. You are going to make these very severe classifications. Here's a quotation for instance.

> THE LEAST important part of Mind gets our almost undivided attention. The illusion-attacked conscious ego—an illusion itself—forces us to see and hear the sense world, or its own vain thought-forms and dream-images, almost all the time. The real part of the Mind is ignored and left out as if it were illusory!
>
> (v6, 8:4.5)

ANTHONY: I would call the higher part of the mind what you're referring to as the Witness, the permanent, and it can infiltrate right into that ego consciousness providing that you went through those three disciplines. And it can be available to you.

RG: OK, so is it that the ego has purified itself and now you speak about the ego as rational?

ANTHONY: No, I wouldn't go that far. I would say that there would be occasions while you're going through those disciplines when it is available to you, but it won't be always available. Nor can you control it. The reason won't always be pure. There's a fluidity of the subjectivity.

RG: But when it's operating in this quest to understand what the nature of the ego is—in that case, it's not the ego that's understanding, it's the rational soul that's understanding what the ego is.

ANTHONY: That could be, sure. There could be insights coming in. But it all comes down to this: You're the battlefield.

FRD: Is that what you mean when you say the ego is the field of experience?

ANTHONY: No, I don't want you to change it. I want you to leave it the way I said it. *You are the battlefield.*

NOTES

1. For more on this idea, see chapter 3, pp. 158–183.

2. See also pages 187–188.

3. See *Perspectives*, p. 153, #5 and p. 330, #3.

4. Not "intellectual" in the modern academic sense, but rather in the sense of "abiding in the Divine Intellect and thus empowered by spiritual wisdom."

5. See Paul Brunton's *The Wisdom of the Overself*, Chapter XIV, for "A Meditation on the Past" and "A Meditation on the Future."

6. Anthony conceived each of the 360 degrees of the zodiac as representing a unique idea or tendency in the universal mind. The positions of the planets at an individual's birth indicate which of these ideas/tendencies will be emphasized in the present phase of that individual's development. The planets represent the powers of the individual mind that will activate/ unfold them. For more on this approach, see chapter 3, pp. 158–183.

ANTHONY DAMIANI
(1922–1984)

■

WHAT WE commonly think of as constituting
the "I" is an idea which changes from year to
year. This is the personal "I." But what we feel
most intimately as being always present in all
these different ideas of the "I," that is, the sense
of being, of existence, never changes at all. It is
this which is our true enduring "I."

(v6, 8:2.1)

IT IS NOT quite correct to assume that we are the
manifested forms of the perfection from which
we emanate. More precisely, we are projections
of a denser medium from the universal mind,
appearing by some catalytic process in natural
sequence within that medium. The cosmic
activity provides each such entity-projection
with an individual life and intelligence centre
through an evolutionary process, whereby its
own volitional directive energies are, ultimately,
merged with the cosmic will in perfect unity
and harmony.

(v6, 8:1.131)

CHAPTER THREE

EGO, OVERSELF, AND WORLD-IDEA

THE EGO is a structure which has been built up in former lives from tendencies, habits, and experiences in a particular pattern. But in the end the whole thing is nothing but a thought, albeit a strong and continuing thought. (v6, 8:2.44)

HS: It's problematical. All you have is these thoughts, and then there's this one thought. I don't understand how one thought could take over a whole stream, so to say.

ANTHONY: How is thought, which is a self-actualizing process, ego?

HS: There would have to be in these self-actualizing thoughts a particular kind of thought.

ANTHONY: All the former tendencies that you have are actualizing themselves as this thought . . .

HS: . . . each instant. And yet there seems to be something within this thought itself that takes itself to be, to actually *be*, real.

ANTHONY: Very good. If you keep going on, what would be the consequences? Wouldn't you see yourself as a phantom? What you take yourself to be is nothing but this process of thought, actualizing itself—this combustion process going on all the time.

HS: At this point it would seem that you relativize the actual existence.

ANTHONY: Stop and examine your life very, very seriously. Like Socrates recommended, the unexamined life is not worth living. So stop and examine it, see what you come up with. You said it. That's what the ego is.

HS: I was going to say it's a cancer.

ANTHONY: That might be a good comparison. It feeds on itself.

HS: So there's this dynamic structure and somehow within that the possibility arises for something in that dynamism, that motion, that structure to take itself to be—to appropriate—the reality of its principle.

ANTHONY: Let's use the example of when you're having a dream. And this dream has 108 scenes, one scene following upon the other. In each scene, scene 1, scene 2, scene 3, there's a continuity of thought. Each thought takes itself to be real, ultimate, actual; but when you look at the dream, you know that the dream character borrowed whatever consciousness he or she has from the person having the dream. It isn't his consciousness, but that consciousness which he has borrowed, that suffuses all his thinking. This is what he calls his ego.

HS: In the analogy, is the character in the dream told that he is in a dream?

ANTHONY: No, the dream character doesn't say, "I'm dreaming." Everything is real for the dream character—including himself. Upon his reality depends the whole of the dream scenario. Aren't we saying that he reappears incessantly, scene after scene?

HS: OK. And in this reappearing he starts to gain a conviction that there's a reality to his reappearing. That in scene 107, scene 108, the same guy would be there? He experiences this continuity of himself in the dream.

ANTHONY: Which he mistakes for identity. The consciousness of the dreamer is immanent in the dream character, but the dream character is going to think it's his consciousness.

AH: Where is the person you know? You described to Herb [HS] this process of the ego with these thoughts that congregate around an idea of continuity.

ANTHONY: Insofar as there is an incessant process of thinking going on, and this thinking that's going on is actualized as Herb, and thinks that it is Herb, always refers to Herb, Herb is going to believe in the reality of his ego. Just think about it for a minute, what you call your identity is this constant, incessant, uninterrupted process of one thought following another.

AH: But they're all strung on some . . .

ANTHONY: ON WHAT!?

AH: On a sense of continuity.

ANTHONY: What's that sense of continuity?

AH: It's empty.

ANTHONY: The sense of continuity is that consciousness which suffuses the dream character and the scenario that's going on.

So we have this dynamic process of combustion, which is an actualizing of one's own thinking into some pseudo-entity. The Buddhists would say there is no substratum to that, there is no consciousness there. The Vedantists would say there *is* an underlying consciousness there. The underlying consciousness for the Vedantists would be the true "I"—the Soul.

For the Buddhist there isn't anything there, so for the Buddhist it becomes like a blank phenomena—there is *no unity*, there is no identity, there is only this continuity, one scene after the other. And if you can find an "I" there, they say, go ahead and do so. The Vedantists say well, what is it that makes it seem as though I am the self-identical person from moment to moment? And they would fall back on consciousness as the substratum of that whole scenario. In other words, for the Vedantist the person having the dream has his consciousness immanent in the whole process and that provides the underlying continuity or the substratum. And the Buddhists would say there isn't anyone there having the dream, that it's just one scene after another going on.

AB: Isn't there an indication in the quote that one scene is the product of all the previous scenes?

ANTHONY: Yes, so that there's this ongoing process where all the previous tendencies are in the next scene, and then all of that in the next. So they call that the snowball effect. As you roll a snowball it gets bigger and bigger, so all these previous tendencies are already present in this moment here and now. No one could dispute that, and no one could prove it.

FDS: But Anthony, along the lines of what you said about the difference between Buddhism and Vedanta—in a sense hasn't PB synthesized their perspectives in the quote where he says that the substratum, the Overself, is really not of the same order or on the same plane as the ego?

ANTHONY: Yes. Neither is the person who's having the dream of the same order as the dream character who imagines his unity.

AB: If you said that consciousness or this awareness is infused into the dream, then the dream subject has this sense of himself. If that consciousness was not infused in the dream person, the dream could still go on, but it would be experienced as other than oneself rather than as one's experience. In this analogy, if you realized that you were dreaming, you could watch that whole process of one scene unfolding into another, without thinking that that was you.

ANTHONY: But then you'd have to say you're bifurcating your consciousness. On one hand you're the dream character and on the other you're witnessing the dream. But if you could keep that conception, then you would have this fluid notion of mind that you have to work with.

In other words, there isn't a wall between the consciousness in the dream character and the consciousness of the person having the dream. There is a fluidity of that consciousness which is in both. And you'll say that the consciousness that the dream character has is the lower consciousness, or the lower mind, and the person having the dream—that's the higher mind. So this way you don't break it up into two things.[1]

RD: The dream character's state of consciousness is distinct from the dream's consciousness.

ANTHONY: You have to *distinguish* them, that's true, but if you *separate* them you're going to be in a lot of trouble. We could put it very simply. What consciousness *is* outside of the imagination is experienced quite differently inside the imagination. But we have to keep the continuity of consciousness, otherwise we're going to have two minds. And mentalism[2] as a theoretical and practical philosophical tradition will just fall apart.

FDM: Can the ego look at itself? I mean, when I examine myself, is the examining I the ego?

ANTHONY: Again, it depends to what extent the person is identified with the ego. A lot of people will make the claim that their ego is objective, that they can see it. Like for instance the remark is made that the ego is non-existent. Do you believe that the ego would ever say that? If you do you're a fool, because the ego will never say that. So you're doing one of two things: Either you're parroting—in other words you read something and you're throwing it back at someone else—or you actually had the experience of seeing its unreality. So which one are you saying? Are you parrotting or are you speaking from experience? See, that's why I can't answer.

FDM: Well insofar as I do try to meditate once in a while, I am trying to look.

ANTHONY: And most of the time you're caught within that whirling thought. You're caught within the ego structure itself, and occasionally there are flashes where you can see yourself objectively. But when you see yourself objectively, you're *not* the ego—otherwise you can't see yourself objectively. And those flashes, those momentary glimpses of truth, are not that rare. They come up very often when you study, when you try very hard; the moment you relax you'll see something—then it's gone, and the ego is right behind.

IT IS LUDICROUS if that part of the mind which is only within the personal consciousness, the ego, sets itself up to deny the Mind-in-itself—its own very Source. For the ego is shut in what it experiences and knows—a much limited area. (v6, 8:1.103)

ANTHONY: That's pretty straightforward. We said that the ego is a bundle of thoughts. Take one thought at a time—the light that suffuses through that thought is caught in it. That's your personal mind. That personal mind now denies its own source, and it's restricted by the scope of that thought within which it is encompassed. If you understand that, you'll get an insight into what the ego is.

RG: So it's in this sense you're saying that the ego is thought, or the identification with thought.

ANTHONY: Well, maybe something like this. We spoke of the ego as thought, a bundle of thoughts, an indefinite number of thoughts, a matrix of thoughts. Take one thought and the light suffuses it. Now light is infinite, all right? But it suffuses that one thought. The light that's captured or encompassed by that one thought is now what you call your personal mind, your ego. The consciousness which is included in that thought for the momentary duration of its existence considers itself as distinct from the source, and even different than the source.

This mind considers itself as distinct from and other than the light from which it comes. And further it is restricted in scope, in comprehension, by the very boundaries of the thought within which it is encased.

DB: The light shines on the thought, and all of a sudden, the thought takes itself to be . . .

ANTHONY: Instead of using the word "thought," use the word "psyche." Any living organism, if it had consciousness infused within it, would think that it is that consciousness. You have to go to living, vital analogies because it wouldn't work with a machine, even a computer. Although I know some people would disagree, a computer doesn't have any self-identity in this way. But a living psyche which had consciousness suffusing it would take itself to be a subject.

> HIS FIRST mental act is to think himself into being. He is the maker of his own "I." This does not mean that the ego is his own personal invention alone. The whole world-process brings everything about, including the ego and the ego's own self-making.
>
> (v6, 8:2.15 AND *Perspectives*, P. 104)

ANTHONY: That's mentalism in a nutshell. That's the whole mentalistic doctrine. The Soul has for its content the World-Idea, and it actualizes that or projects that World-Idea out from within itself. And included in that World-Idea is the ego and the process that it's going to go through.

RC: That word "His" here seems to be more than just the ego, isn't it?

ANTHONY: That "His" is Soul, Oversoul or Soul identified with Nature.

MB: Can the Overself think itself into being?

ANTHONY: As your ego is evolving, the world is evolving with it. Think of the whole World-Idea as contained within each individual Soul. Each individual Soul projects the World-Idea, but first it has to have the intermediary of an ego through which the world gets projected. All that exists within the Overself, within the Soul itself. So that's really the kernel of mentalism in that one sentence. He's just stating it as briefly and tersely as he can. And you can see the status of the ego in that framework: The ego has a definite role and it has to fulfill that role before it can realize what the Source of Being is for it. So when he says that it creates being, or the Soul produces sensible being for itself through which it is going to manifest, he is really speaking about mentalism.

MB: We were talking about the ego as being a thought, but it seems to make sense to further characterize this thought as both passive and active. It's not merely the product of something, but it also has a role to play.

ANTHONY: Yes, it's both potential and actual at one and the same time. That's why I tell you to think of it as a matrix of possibilities, always in the process of actualizing themselves. But you can't conceive of the matrix as being actualized at any time.

THE "I" is *not* a thought at all. It is the very principle of Consciousness itself, pure Being. It is neither personal mind nor physical body, neither ego nor little self. Without it they could not exist or function. It is their witness.   (v6, 8:1.72)

HE: He's talking about the I there, not the I-thought, and they're different, right?

RC: Yes.

ANTHONY: So what does he mean here by "I"?

HS: I would say that he means the Overself.

ANTHONY: Yes, OK. Discussion's over, right?

HS: No, actually, to be honest, I have no idea what that

means. I don't know what it means to be the principle of consciousness in itself.

ANTHONY: Well, there no one can help you. But at least verbally you're capable of distinguishing that what he's referring to as the "I" is also equivalent to speaking about the Overself or Soul. The Soul is the principle. So what he's saying is: Don't think of the "I" as the process of combustion, think of the "I" as Soul.

The nature of the Soul's consciousness is unchanging. What about the nature of the ego? It's changing from instant to instant. That's manifestation of the world. You've got to put these two together. That's the crux of the whole argument that's going on.

Soul in its nature or essence is of an unchanging consciousness. The ego, which is part of the World-Idea, is constantly changing from moment to moment. You've got to explain that.

You've got to explain the Buddhist position *and* the Vedantic position. One is a psychological one and the other is more metaphysical. Understand the nature of the consciousness that the ego represents—that is from moment to moment, and that would be the Buddhist position. Understand the nature of the consciousness which is always abiding, never changing, and that would be the Vedantic position.

Now the two of them are together in every and any situation that you care to think about. We know of only the one that's always changing. We don't know about the unchanging. Now if you want to get to this matter you have to understand this interrelationship of these two.

AH: Is "embodied soul" equatable to ego?

ANTHONY: I think by embodied soul they're speaking about one part of the soul, or something which is given off by the soul which permeates or pervades or takes possession of some part of the World-Idea which we say is a body. It then identifies with that body and that combination is what they're calling the conjoint, if I follow what they've been saying.

On one hand, the body and everything that we recognize to be a vehicle is something which is produced by ideation— the World-Mind's ideation—and that's going on instant to instant. The Buddhists will explain everything from that principle, OK? And then there's the other point of view that speaks about the soul whose essence or whose consciousness is always abiding, never changing. That is, so to speak, the point of view that the Vedantists are coming from. So that seems to be more psychological. Whereas the Buddhist's position would be to talk about the World-Idea being manifested from instant to instant, and that seems to be very metaphysical. And it's these two—the combination of the metaphysical and the psychological—which is the underlie of our discussion. Bring it out in the open. See if we can see what we're talking about. It's tremendously fascinating.

KD: You said the soul provides what's permanent. And then it's the ego that is changing moment to moment. I don't see that. I see where it could be the light of the soul that would be the permanent part and it's the World-Idea that would be the changing part.

ANTHONY: Same thing. That's what I said. The body is part of the world, right? And the world is changing from instant to instant. So my body is changing along with it, from instant to instant. So the ego, or the body, that's changing from instant to instant. But the illuminating light that comes in from the soul, that's not changing. That's not part of the World-Idea. It's illuminating the body which is part of the World-Idea. So that's self-abiding. That's unchanging.

KD: But we said before that the ego is this combination, this conjoint.

ANTHONY: Yes, yes. We're saying the ego, which includes the body, is what's constantly changing from moment to moment. That doesn't have consciousness which doesn't change. If we say that the World-Idea—the world and all the bodies in it—is the product of this Mind which, from instant to instant, is manifesting the world, then body and the world have to be changing from moment to moment. And we're speaking about consciousness. I'm speaking about this body which is manifesting from instant to instant. I'm speaking about consciousness manifesting from instant to instant. It's consciousness. It's the consciousness of this greater mind that is projecting the world from instant to instant. That means that my body is this consciousness manifesting instant to instant. Inside that—and this is a colloquialism—inside that is this light of the soul which doesn't change. This is the light, so to speak, that becomes aware of change. It itself is unchanging. And I've got these two things together.

KD: You just made a difference. You said the consciousness manifesting the world moment by moment is different from the awareness of that light that's lighting that up.

ANTHONY: Exactly! The unchanging consciousness within the changing consciousness. Or if you want to put it the other way around, I don't care. But you have these two together.

KD: And that's what has to be . . .

ANTHONY: That's what you have to understand.

KD: The soul's nature is constituted of this dual nature, the consciousness that brings the world moment by moment . . .

ANTHONY: No, no, no. The nature of the soul's consciousness is abiding. It doesn't change. The continuity and identity of the subjective factor has to remain all the time. You don't get rid of that.

RG: Given that background, the question is still there. This soul is twofold: the unchanging light which is eternal and is always what it is, and this emanent which is associated with the World-Idea.

ANTHONY: There you're not speaking about the twofold-ness of its essence.

RG: You're not?

ANTHONY: No. Is the essence twofold?

RG: I don't think so.

ANTHONY: No, the essence is identical. This embodying soul, what we speak about as embodying soul, its essence must be that of the nature of the transcendent.

AS: One essence of soul.

ANTHONY: Yes, one essence. The essence is one.

THE BODY is in reality an object for the mind, which is its subject; and not only the body, but also whatever the ego thinks or feels becomes an object, too. It is less easy to see and even more necessary to understand that this ego, this subject, is itself an object to a higher part of the mind.   (v6, 8:2.67)

AH: What does it mean to talk about an experience of ego as object? Isn't the description of that experience itself from the point of view of the ego?

ANTHONY: Don't have too rigid a concept of conscious-ness or mind. This higher mind is also present within the ego. You could think of it that way. In other words, don't compartmentalize mind. If you think of three bulbs, one within the other, and there is light traversing all three bulbs, we would say the innermost bulb is your ego consciousness, the next one outer would be a higher witnessing conscious-ness, the next one beyond that is even a higher consciousness. But don't make this break or hiatus too rigid or you'll say, "Well who's experiencing the ego?" You'll encapsulate it in that first bulb.

DD: If you describe this intermingling in our day-to-day experience, wouldn't you say that we drift in and drift out of relative amounts of egoness and egolessness?

ANTHONY: Yes, basically that's what we're saying. Very often there could be a higher awareness in a person, but because of his habitual modes of being he's not even aware. It's right there. It requires a little discernment and practice to be able to distinguish that there are times when the ego is objective to you—all its thoughts, feelings, and everything. At that moment you have to pin it down and realize that you are the higher awareness, but most of us don't do that.

> ALL OUR thoughts necessarily exist in the successive-
> ness of time, but the thought of the ego is a more
> complicated affair and exists also in time and space,
> because the body is part of the ego. Whatever we do,
> the ego as such will continue its existence. But we
> need not identify ourselves with it; we can put
> some distance between us and it. The more we
> do so, the more impersonal we shall become,
> and vice versa.
>
> (v6, 8:2.49)

ANTHONY: What's the point here?

HS: Generally thoughts are spoken of as in time, and body is a peculiar kind of thought which has spatial reference.

ANTHONY: So you could have a succession of thoughts and they're not in space. Once more, how about the body?

HS: Body necessarily, by definition, is a spatial entity.

ANTHONY: It's a corporealization of thought. Then you have to have it in space.

LR: Doesn't he say that the ego exists in time and space?

HS: In time as thought, in time and space as thought embodied.

AH: Body necessitates the spatial reference, but does egoity?

ANTHONY: Isn't egoity a thought? Is egoity a body? Or let's separate egoism from ego. When I speak about your egoism, am I speaking about your body or about your glorification of the identity you assume between this consciousness and the body? If you think of a person's egoism, is it something that's spatial?

AS: No, of course not.

ANTHONY: Well, then, it's thought. With any kind of thought you have, one follows after the other, unless you get three at a time. I mean, I notice one comes and then another and then another. And even in those people who have tremendous facility to employ four secretaries and keep them all busy at the same time, they still have to get to one point at a time. Thought is successive—one follows after the other.

Now, if you were just pure thought, I wouldn't be able to find you any place in space. But now suppose as thought you also corporealize yourself, like when you think something real intensely it will appear in front of you. You spatialize it, you make an image out of it. Now you have to refer to space, and the ego has these two aspects, a spatial and a temporal aspect.

CONSCIOUSNESS ordinarily believes itself to be limited to the physical body. This belief it calls "I," it claims to be the "I." That they are associated together is unquestionable. But further enquiry will yield a further and startling result: it functions *through* the body and to that extent the connection gives life to the body, thus creating the belief that it is the body when in reality it only permeates it. What happens is that a part (the body) is imposing itself upon the whole (the consciousness).

(v6, 8:1.85)

ANTHONY: All you have to do is go back to the chapter "The Birth of the Universe" in PB's *The Wisdom of the Overself.*

ME: He seems to be speaking of individual consciousness here, not the consciousness fabricating this body, right?

ANTHONY: He's not explaining how the all-encompassing intelligence or Oversoul produces from within itself the body through which it is going to operate. He's only explaining that this consciousness associates with a body, permeates that body, and now that body thinks itself to be, as you said, a self-independent reality.

If you go back to the dream analogy, I think the point he's bringing in is that the dream character that appears to be a living reality is so because it is permeated by the consciousness of the person who's having the dream. The question as to whether the dream character is fabricated by the intelligence that's having the dream isn't brought in here. The point is that the body with this life in it takes itself to be the whole.

AH: But there is something of the whole there, insofar as it is alive.

ANTHONY: How is there something of the whole of the Overself in the body?

AH: Because consciousness permeates the body.

ANTHONY: I'm glad you name me a Buddha—that was easy! How is the whole in the body? How is the stupendous wisdom of the Overself here now present? It's a misconception—the ego or this light associated with the body says, "I am It." That's the danger—everyone assumes that his ego is the principle of reality for himself because of that misconception.

WHAT HE calls the "I" does not get reborn in further bodies, as he believes, nor did it do so in the past. But it does appear to do so. Only deep analytical thought associated with mystical meditation can de-mesmerize him from his self-made idea. (v6, 8:1.231)

ANTHONY: The question is: "How could the Overself ever

incarnate? How could Being incarnate?" Basically, the criticism is against any animistic understanding of reincarnation. I'm Joe Doe, and when I come back Joe Doe becomes Henry Smith. There's this notion of some sort of continuity, and he's knocking all that out. That's not what reincarnation is. Reincarnation is really misunderstood by anyone who thinks that the same principle, the Soul, is actually in the body.

The way we understand it is that Soul is an indivisible whole of which part—the reasoning part of the Soul—projects and makes actualizations in the imagination of the possibilities that are contained within that indivisible whole. But in itself Soul is the principle and never could reincarnate.

He just wants to knock that out, in case you have any idea that you're immortal because you keep reincarnating. That goes out the window, too. For a lot of people that is a kind of feeling of immortality, that they're going to be coming back. But what's coming back is not you.

LR: Isn't the point also that the Overself never gets reborn because it's never born at all?

ANTHONY: Yes.

LR: The Overself would have to be present to every incarnation, but it is never getting born or reborn.

ANTHONY: Well, it all follows from when we pointed out that the light suffuses this matrix of thoughts or possibilities. It is those thoughts or possibilities actualizing themselves as various entities; it is not the light which suffuses them that incarnates. It's thoughts themselves getting actualized, not that light, and so there can't be an incarnation of that principle.

In other words, the I never incarnated, now or before, nor will it do so in the future. So what is all this talk about reincarnation? He says you're going to have to give it a lot of thought. You're going to have to try to get some experience in meditation to understand. But reincarnation is just another word, most people don't know what they're talking about.

LR: Is there an appearance of the I?

ANTHONY: If the I is an eternal and immutable principle, how could a matrix of possibilities be an appearance of it? How can the ego reincarnate if it's a matrix of possibilities? And the Soul cannot reincarnate because it's the principle of being.

AS: So what does incarnate?

ANTHONY: He's saying you have to go figure this out!

IT WOULD be an error to believe that it is the Overself which reincarnates. It does not. But its offspring—the ego—does.   (V6, 8:1.232 AND *Perspectives*, P. 106)

ANTHONY: Do you understand what he's saying? Is *this* ego, John Doe, going to come back again?

VM: The tendencies that are manifesting as the ego in this life, remanifest in terms of another ego that has some characteristics which are similar.

ANTHONY: Yes, but tendencies aren't self-identical. They are only a matrix. They can be combined in a variety of ways, although usually they can be pretty persistent too.

The point here is to recognize that the ego as such is *no permanent entity*, to begin with. And therefore when this passes on, when the body passes on, is decomposed, those tendencies are decomposed. Now what is it that will manifest the next time? It will certainly be some of those tendencies that were in that prior ego. And you will be the heir of the deeds of that ego. But you will not be that ego. You'll be something other than that ego. An animistic conception of reincarnation is being denied. John Doe does not come back and exist as John Doe again. Nor does the Overself incarnate, because that's not possible.

Let's do something like this. We take a test tube and fill it up with a lot of dust particles and keep them in motion, and then we shine a searchlight in that test tube. Each one of these dust particles is going to be saying "I" and that "I" is going to be borrowed from the light that's shining through it. Now, of all those dust particles, which one do you think is going to reincarnate the next time?

RG: None of those dust particles.

TS: Or all of them.

ANTHONY: In a sense, all of them, insofar as you recapitulate all that you've been in the past.

RS: The definition of ego that we give as a matrix of thoughts is for as long as we are living individuals. Next time all those thoughts are based upon all those previous tendencies.

ANTHONY: In other words, it's like a snowball effect. And the snowball gets bigger and bigger. Did you ever take a snowball and roll it down a hill, and as it goes down it gets bigger and bigger? This is basically what we're talking about, because to think of any ego entity incarnating is a sheer form of animism.

I'm trying to explain this quote, and also many others where he hammers away at the fact that the ego is no static entity. The way he has just explained it I think is good. If you think of it as these habitual tendencies, they become cumulative, they go on building up. There is no entity there in the sense that there is a thing which is permanent and static, but you could think of it in the sense of an entity if you keep in mind that it's an ongoing process that never stops. And then when you start saying, "Well, what incarnates?" we immediately understand that you misunderstood. Because there's *no entity* that's going to reincarnate. Tony is not going to come back. When he's dead he's *dead*. All the parts that went to make him are going to be dispersed.

RG: Why do you define entity as only the manifested Tony? Why are you limiting your idea of entity to that?

ANTHONY: By "entity" I'm limiting it to anything that I know as a thought. That's what I'm referring to as the entity. Everything that I can speak about in terms of Tony is always a thought.

RG: Are there relatively permanent thoughts?

ANTHONY: Relatively permanent? Yes, you could say that they go on for a while, sure. But certainly if you look back twenty years ago, you see that there's hardly the same person there anymore, and the person that we're referring to is of course an ongoing mental process, a combustion process that's going on all the time. Death won't stop it.

FD: Before you said: You take this matrix of possibilities, now each life is a different arrangement, a crystallization of these possibilities.

ANTHONY: Tell me, in this life that you're living, you're adding to it, right? And the next life you're adding to it.

FD: Yes, but I'm essentially the same person I was twenty years ago.

ANTHONY: No, you're not! If by person you mean ego.

FD: By person, I mean identity.

ANTHONY: That's another thing! The identity is that light which permeates the ego, is always self-identical with itself; but what it permeates is not self-identical with itself. The identity always refers to the subject, the miracle of subjectivity, which is never to be confused with the object of that subjectivity. The object of that subjectivity is thought. Thought in its totality is what you call your ego. This thought now appropriates the light coming into it and says, "I am I," which is a downright lie. The "I" is the *light* and not the light penetrating through the dust. The dust isn't light!

FD: The subject always seems to have the same way of appropriating the different contents.

ANTHONY: The subject never appropriates anything. The *content*, the ego, appropriates the light and says, "I am this identity. I am the ego, I am the reality, I am the Self." That's exactly what is *not* the Self.

RG: But that's a pretty permanent thought.

ANTHONY: No, because it's different every other instant. Whereas the light of the Soul that he's speaking about is *never* different from moment to moment. There is no interval in it!

FD: It's appropriating the same light every lifetime.

ANTHONY: The light is always the same.

FD: But the contents have altered from moment to moment. Today I'm black but I'm appropriating this light and I'm saying this is me; tomorrow I'm purple, I'm appropriating this light and I'm saying this is me . . .

ANTHONY: Which is the me? Is the me the black and the purple?

FD: I'm identifying with what I'm appropriating.

ANTHONY: No, you're not! You say that you're the light, I say that's bones! [*laughter*] You don't think of yourself as the light of consciousness, never in a million years. But what else could you think of yourself as? Thought. If you don't want to say thought, then say the physical body. I don't care what terms you use, I'm just coming from the mentalistic framework that the only thing you could know is thought. You can't know anything else. But if you want to say, "I am the physical body," fine. It's the physical body, the ego saying, "I am the Self." The Self doesn't say "I am the Self." It never will.

AS: It's a funny paradox and that's why it's so hard to say "reincarnation," because the ego incarnates but it doesn't reincarnate. And what's permanent, the light, never incarnates at all.

ANTHONY: Thank you very much, that's perfect.

CA: It's the very self-grasping of any thought, this appropriation, that makes reincarnation happen, propels that tendency to arise again. So reincarnation itself is the very propulsive force, or leftover force, of this self-grasping in any thought.

RG: Is there an organization of all incarnations? Prior to the manifestation of the incarnation?

ANTHONY: No. The organization, the intelligibility, or the essential *daimon* governing over all the incarnations is not the same. There is no way of making an analogy there.

EC: Anthony, I can see me not coming back as Eleanor but how about PB, doesn't he come back pretty much as that developed soul?

ANTHONY: Anyone who is born into a physical body has to go through the search of finding himself all over again. Remember, the first link of the *nidana* chain[3] is *avidya* [ignorance]. He has got to go into a physical body, he's got to get acquainted with the brain, he has to go through the whole mess like everybody else. He may be perfectly aware of who he is and what he is until that moment when he is in the body. As far as I know, there is no awareness in the sense of an unbroken thread of continuity of Soul awareness. It's broken when you are born. Then you have to institute the search for self discovery. In the case of a sage, of course, it's more immediate, and the prevalence is something that is obvious to those that are spiritually oriented. But everyone has to go through that. I might make the exception of the avatar, but I don't understand anything about avatars.

RG: What happened to the celestial ray of the Overself and the differentiation of one Overself from another as this historical relationship to the Overself which does transcends one manifestation? Where does that fit in?

ANTHONY: Yes, I don't disagree with that.

RG: I don't understand. How does that idea fit in with the non-reincarnation of an entity and just this bundle of energy that manifests? If there is a certain historical relation to an Overself that obviously transcends one life, it must have some unique relationship to the Overself. It's neither the Overself nor one particular manifestation, so how do you talk about that? Can't you speak of that ray as what is reincarnated?

ANTHONY: I don't see why you can't speak of it that way and still keep the truth of what we're saying. In other words, if we think of an ego as an ongoing process of thought, without interruption, and constantly manifesting itself, then you have this bundle of possibilities, this matrix of thoughts, which is constantly in the flesh. Now, I don't see what objection there could be to saying that there is a historical relationship of the Overself to all these series of incarnations.

If you speak about the thread-soul, the *sutra atma* which flows through all of them—again, that's the identity we're speaking about. That's identity, that's self-identity.

RG: Isn't there a distinction between the awareness of that identity and the content side, which seems to be the distinct historical manifestation of that being?

ANTHONY: I'll still say the same thing. There is, let's say, a *sutra atma*, a thread of unity that underlies a series of incarnations. So you have from life one to life ten the same *atma* underlying all of those incarnations. In other words, it's the same light going into each one of those ten test tubes. There will be nothing wrong with saying that. The point I'm simply trying to get at is that there is no self-identity in each one of those test tubes.

RG: When taken as distinct test tubes, I agree with you.

ANTHONY: Well, in that case there can't be anything reincarnating. And I think the remark made was quite exact. We can speak about something incarnating but not reincarnating. There are a lot of romantic ideals and mistaken notions about reincarnation, because the way it's generally spoken of is really quite animistic. It's not mature thinking. It's kind of primitive to believe that I'm going to come back again, and this time instead of AD, as AJD, and the next time AJSD, as long as AD keeps coming back. No, AD does not come back.

This throw of the dice, this potential, these possibilities, will not constitute you again. Just from an elementary acquaintance with the astrological chart, you see that that can't be. .

ME: It's not entirely random, though.

ANTHONY: Of course not. I mean, if I spend all my time trying to be a sage, I'm not going to be born a bum.

ME: What provides for this continuum, then?

ANTHONY: The continuity in thought itself. If you think a certain thought, and there's a tendency to repeat the thought, then that thought goes on acquiring a certain momentum of its own. But the thought—the inherited potentialities, the habits that you forge—is not an entity. Let's say that you develop an aura to be isolated and alone, life after life. Well, that tends to repeat itself, naturally. But there's no one there that's incarnating, reincarnating. And as unpleasant as this is, you have to really think about it. Because it's a kind of specious immortality that people seek in reincarnation. It's better that they cut it right off now, and leave it to the others to take that.

I'm the sum of everything that's been in the past. Now add to that this lifetime and all the experiences. This goes on. The next incarnation, add that. And you tell me where there's an entity in all this. But notice, the emphasis here is on continuity, there's a continuity, but what he was speaking about was identity.

So you could think of one as vertical, you could think of the other as horizontal. The Buddhists always speak in terms of continuity. Constant repetition. The *atma* theory of Vedanta is always one of "I." I am what I am. These are the two points of view that we discussed as substance and function. And from our point of view, the two of them have to be brought together or you're going to be either in heaven or hell.

MB: The ego is not the continuity. The incarnation is sort of superimposed on the continuity, so you can't say that anything reincarnates. The incarnation by definition ends when the body ends.

ANTHONY: We can leave it like that, and you'll begin to have an understanding of what reincarnation is. Now that does not exclude the *jataka*[4] and all that, that there can be a memory of past lives. That is not excluded.

RG: It seems to me you're positing the level of *atman*, pure consciousness, and then the next level of the individual you're positing is the manifested corporeal being. Now it seems that there are levels in between that have prior positions in the scale—in between the manifested physical being, or the mental being, and below the *atman*. I want to talk about this type of individual that reincarnates. That's neither the Overself nor . . .

ANTHONY: Even that causal body goes through changes. It's an expediency, and we use it, but even that goes through change.

RG: I don't want to hold to the utter identity of it.

ANTHONY: It could be a long drawn-out thing. That's why it's possible for certain people to recall, distinctly, their past lives. Sure. But what we mean here is that the view that they get is that of thoughts, images from the past, which are retained in that continuum. I'm not explaining the complications in the notion of a thought-continuum. I'm just trying to reduce my answer to the simplicity that this treatment warrants.

AP: If you look at karma as a mere continuum of thought, it just goes on without purpose. But if you think of some intelligence behind the ego which orders the thoughts, that is different.

ANTHONY: We're not discussing that. What we're discussing is the fact that the instantiation that takes place from the realm of the Soul is always one of an ongoing continuity. We're not discussing the fact that there is intelligibility behind that instantiation. I'm trying to hammer home one point now, and that is to deprive you people of an idea that you are immortal because you're going to be reborn again. I want that really understood. Then we'll talk about the intelligibility of the law of karma.

FD: There's an identical consciousness that exists throughout many lives and there's an ongoing continuum of tendencies that seem to stay the same from life to life, adding up and building up.

ANTHONY: Nothing stays the same.

FD: The tendencies?

ANTHONY: They alter, they change. Everything changes. The only thing that doesn't change is change. Everything changes. No one would deny that there is a relative persistence of certain tendencies over a long span of time, yes, but that's not identity.

FD: I'm not saying that it is identity but if those tendencies are relatively the same, then the way I perceive the world is going to be conditioned by those very tendencies. So the consciousness and the perception are pretty much the same in a lot of ways.

ANTHONY: No. Consciousness and perception are not the same.

FD: Perception is the same from life to life if the tendencies stay relatively the same, no?

ANTHONY: I'm not going to disagree with the fact that, relatively, you're going to be perceiving a similar world to the one that you saw yesterday and the day before. I'm not going to doubt those things. I'm just talking about—and I'm trying to emphasize—that the entity that incarnates is no static, permanent thing but an ongoing process. Even in many of your readings you'll get the fact that there's this process of evolution constantly going on and it's spiraling. Sometimes it seems to be lower, sometimes higher. But in that whole process of the manifestation of the World-Idea, there could not possibly be anything permanent in it. That includes the ego

and everything that it thinks, everything that it does, everything that it thought itself to be.

> THERE IS an intermediate entity, compounded of the
> ego's best part and the point of contact with the
> Overself. Call it the higher mind, the conscience, or the
> intellectual intuition, if you wish. (v14, 22:1.7)

ANTHONY: He's speaking about the middle section. He's
speaking about the Witness I. That's the intermediary between the Soul and the empirical personality.

AH: Is that intermediary point a way of speaking of close
proximity to the bare givenness of I AM?

ANTHONY: Yes, and it could lean in either direction. The
reasoning soul, or the highest phase of the soul—not the intellectual Soul itself, because there is no reasoning there—
can lean towards *that* [the I AM], or it could lean towards
the empirical.

AH: What would be an example of the best part of the ego?
Behavior in accordance with philosophic ideals?

ANTHONY: Yes.

> THE LITTLE EGO is the only being he knows: the greater
> Being of philosophic Consciousness would be, and is,
> beyond his comprehension. (v6, 8:1.25)

PC: From the point of view of the circle of thought that
the ego is, it couldn't understand about that consciousness
because you can't understand it through thought.

ANTHONY: What we're trying to do in some of the classes
is to explain the nature of this Being, to see that it has various
ways of understanding, that it has direct cognition into itself,
that it can also develop a critical faculty of understanding
the World-Idea which is manifesting, and that within that

there would be these various levels of intellection, rationality, mentation. We've been trying to show what the philosophic conception of what we are is in comparison to what the ego thinks we are. The ego has this opinion, "This is what I am," whereas what we've been trying to understand is: "What is the philosophic conception of what we are?" The ego can't even conceive of these things.

That's why I always preface with the remark, when we're reading or studying people like PB, to remember that they're coming from the philosophic understanding of what a man is, what he's capable of, and the extent of his true being. Whereas just think of what the ego thinks it is; we can see that it can't get out of that notion of what it thinks it is. It's caught in that notion; it lives in that notion. But the philosophic conception says, "Look! You're even capable of contemplating the Void, the ultimate reality."

> How is it that I am—and know that I am—substantially the same man today as yesterday, that I remember the happenings of a year ago? The answer must be that there is a continuous self, or being, or mind, in me, distinct from its thoughts or experiences.   (v6, 8:1.97)

ANTHONY: There is an underlying consciousness which is self-identical with itself. He didn't say it was thought that remembered itself. In other words, the Buddhist explanation would be that it is thought that remembers a previous thought and is a thought, so to speak, in its own right: Each thought-moment contains the possibility of a recollection of its prior activity, or prior whatever. But what PB is saying is that you have these two streams, or let's say a juxtaposition: the evolving stream of thought, which we're calling the ego, and a light which permeates that evolving stream of thought and is constantly there. Now the Buddhists explain memory or self-identity in terms of the self-continuing stream of thought. PB is not doing that. He's saying no, the identity belongs to the person, the one who is underlying that stream of thought, and it's not to be confused with the stream of thought.

AH: In that quote, Anthony, what does he call that underlying consciousness?

ANTHONY: The Overself. That's the higher self. That's what tethers together the stream of thoughts, the continuum that is constantly changing.

AH: Does this consciousness that underlies thought, that allows memory to be possible, transcend one life?

ANTHONY: Oh yes, that's self-identical.

AH: Does it have a relationship with the I?

ANTHONY: It *is* the basis for the feeling of I that you have.

AH: But it's in no way associated with any kind of personal I.

ANTHONY: No. It is the *basis* of the personal I that you feel.

AH: But in itself it's not personal.

ANTHONY: No.

FD: Why can't the very tendencies themselves which make up the person be spoken of as the identity, the person, and not the light?

ANTHONY: If by person you mean the ego self, yes. You can speak about that as his identity, but would you be satisfied with that?

FD: No, but if I think of this consciousness lighting up this matrix of thoughts, why *can't* the previous cause be inherent in each effect? Then you don't have to speak of the consciousness as lighting this up.

ANTHONY: First of all, it is that light penetrating into the psyche which is the basis for your supposition that you are an I, a real I. It is not the psyche's functioning in terms of itself that would ever come out and say "I am I." It's not inherent in thought itself to conceive of itself as a subject, it's inherent in the light which permeates that thought.[5] And another reason why thought couldn't be an I is because it's not permanent, it's going through a constant process of change from moment to moment.

FD: Yes, but the previous moment is continually present, in a way.

ANTHONY: The whole point being made there is that you won't find any identity in one thought, and in the next thought following that. You'll find some sort of discontinuous continuity, but not an I. And you have to discriminate between the thought and the subject of that thought. And in this case the ego and its thought are both objects to that consciousness. It's in that consciousness that you get the feeling of I; you don't get it from the psychical processes.

FD: I hear that, but I can't really say that I'm the same person every day; there's somewhat of an identity, but there's some difference too.

ANTHONY: What is the difference, the fact that you're a day older? If that's the difference, you're speaking about the entirety of everything that's objective. In other words, if you think of yourself as different, you're thinking about something objective, right?

FD: I guess so.

ANTHONY: No. You should be very clear about this.

FD: It would have to be in the contents.

ANTHONY: It would have to be objective. Now, how would a subject that is truly subjective know itself? Can it know itself in that way, through being objective to itself? In any way it can be objective, it can't be you. It can only be, so to speak, some material idea. Some idea—let me leave out the word material. This was exactly the reason why I brought out this discussion.

In that statement, PB made it very clear where he stands as far as the doctrine goes. He points out that thought is, so to speak, going on all the time. The Buddhists say that all we are is these thoughts, one after the other. If you ask them for an explanation of the self-identity of the entity, they would place it in that thought. Now PB is very deliberately pointing out, that's not where your identity is coming from because that thought-following-upon-thought is a mechanical process. He's placing the subjectivity in the Consciousness, and he's making no bones about it.

AH: I don't want to debate the point, but is there no place in thought that you can find that permanent I?

ANTHONY: It's not something you could find, because if it was it would be something objective.

AH: So, as long as you can't find it, why worry about it?

ANTHONY: You're making the test of reality what PB would call the "fingertip philosophy." "I can't find an I, therefore it's not around."

RG: The whole claim of "findable by analysis" predisposes the question to find something that's analytical, and the I is exactly the thing that isn't analytical.

ANTHONY: Let me put it this way to amplify that point. That by which you smell, taste, hear, see, think—how are you going to find it?

■ ■ ■

IT WOULD be wrong to believe that there are two separate minds, two independent consciousnesses within us—one the lower ego-mind, and the other, the higher Overself-mind—with one, itself unwatched, watching the other. There is but one independent illuminating mind and everything else is only a limited and reflected image within it. The ego is a thought-series dependent on it.

(v6, 8:1.74 AND *Perspectives*, P. 103)

IF IT COULD be both that which is observed and the observer itself for a single second then surely the two mental conditions would instantly annihilate each other. The task is as hard and as foredoomed to failure as trying to look directly at one's own face. Thus the inherent impossibility of such a situation stands revealed. There is only one last hope for success in such a quest and that is to abandon all attempts to know it by the ordinary methods of knowledge. What would such an approach necessarily involve? It would involve two factors: first, a union of the personal "I" into the hidden observer, of which it is an expression, although the merger must not be so absolute as to obliterate the ego altogether; second, an abandonment of the intellectual method which breaks up consciousness into separate thoughts. (v6, 8:4.171)

VM: PB says that if that witness consciousness and that apparent subjectivity were to get together, they would some-how annihilate each other. But that approach is foredoomed, you can't go that route. So what route should you take? His answer seems to be a mystical one. The first thing is to absorb that lower subjectivity into the higher, at least temporarily, and also drop the demand to find an intellectual understanding of this paradox—at least in the lower sense of intellectual.

ANTHONY: Can we try the example of dreaming again? You're having the dream, and the dream is a series of thoughts which includes, of course, the presentation of a dream Vic with the dream problems and dream tables and dream chairs. They're discontinuous, but there is a discontinuous continuity, one thought following upon the other. Dream Vic appears in the dream. There's a problem that he's faced with, and he's thinking about the problem in the dream.

Now we're saying that the dream itself is a series of

thoughts, one following upon the other uninterruptedly. We're saying that the consciousness which belongs to the person who is dreaming, who has the dream, is immanent in the dream subject. Now, in some way Vic's consciousness is immanent in dream Vic's consciousness. It isn't that dream Vic and Vic are two different minds or two different consciousnesses. They are one and the same.

PB suggests that if you want to get to the hidden observer, the dream subject identifies himself with his own subjectivity, his consciousness, and if he follows that through he will arrive at the Vic who is having the dream or the consciousness of the hidden observer. If he attempts to get to the observer, the real Vic, through the thoughts that he's having in the dream, it would be hopeless.

If dream Vic in the dream thinks that he can get to Vic's consciousness by debating about it, by having thoughts about it, by conceptualizing about it, it will be a dead end. Just transpose that, just translate that into modern wakeful consciousness.

AH: If the dream Vic looks out to any kind of object, the task is impossible.

ANTHONY: Yes. It can't be done. Only when the dream Vic says, "Wait a minute, maybe I have a real Daddy upstairs somewhere," and he identifies himself with this consciousness which is immanent in dream Vic, and he goes upstairs, will he find the hidden observer.

If you identify with the consciousness that's illuminating the thoughts that you refer to as the ego thoughts, if you identify with the *logos* principle or consciousness within you and not with the thoughts, then you could trace back the genesis of this consciousness to its origin. This would be the hidden observer in you.

The other problem would be this. If dream Vic really had

a consciousness of his own, and the real Vic had his own consciousness, and they confronted each other, it would be sheer cancellation.

vm: Let me see if I understand this by restating it in slightly different language. You do have this higher subjectivity which is this all-encompassing mind, within which this appearance and apparent subjectivity occur. It's impossible to effect the unification of those two apparently opposed positions through the lower route. In other words, you can't make the unification occur on the level of the discursive thought. If this unification is to occur, it's by sublating or negating.

anthony: But you see, it wouldn't be unification. It would be the cessation of dream Vic's identification with something external, but identifying with the immanence of the consciousness that he thinks is his.

The dream is a very good example because in the dream you can see that the consciousness which is immanent in dream Vic is identifying itself with the sensible appearance of a dream Vic, and thinks himself to be those thoughts. So that the thoughts, in a sense, appropriate that consciousness to themselves and think of themselves as an "I" independent of the dreaming, of the real Vic who is having the dream.

vm: The question is: What principle or factor gives rise to the possibility of that limited identification of that larger consciousness with some fragment of the whole? In other words, how does one account for this mistake?

anthony: If it were a principle, then you would make it a reality. But isn't it also possible that insofar as there are thought processes, that within thought processes there is room for error, and this is the error that is being committed by the thought processes? And wouldn't this be the fundamental ignorance?

ah: Is that to say that any kind of split is ignorance?

ANTHONY: There is no split here. There is one mind functioning and there are grades within it, or stratifications within it. There's no split.

AH: Then what is ignorance?

ANTHONY: Well, we just said that there's this primal possibility for thought to misconceive its own operation. To take itself to be a subject! Thought takes itself to be the subject! It has usurped the light and now that light in conjunction with that thought takes itself to be the subject. There is the apparent "two minds."

AH: In taking itself to be the subject, an attempt to solve the problem at the level of thoughts involves an infinite regression.

ANTHONY: Yes, it can only attack the problem by identifying itself with its subjectivity. Another example would be a mote which is passing through a sunbeam: The mote is lit up, and this mote now takes itself to be light—it's lit up by the light and takes itself to be an independent particle of light.

Let's go back to the dream analogy, because I think it's more picturesque. Let's concentrate on the subjectivity. The subjectivity or consciousness which belongs to the dreamer is the same consciousness which is immanent in the dream subject. This consciousness is immanent in the dream subject because it is associated or identified with the appearance of a dream Vic, then this dream Vic appropriates for himself the I, and calls himself the I.

BS: But that appropriation is what we're calling the error.

ANTHONY: Right now we're really concerned with trying to distinguish, and see that this one consciousness cannot be divided into two subjects or two minds.

AH: Please say something about the lines which say, "If it could be both that which is observed and the observer itself for a single second then surely the two mental conditions would instantly annihilate each other."

ANTHONY: That would be the same as saying that if you conceive of dream Vic to have an ultimate consciousness, and real Vic to have an ultimate consciousness, and they were objects to each other, there would be an utter cancellation. Each would be object to each, and each would be subject in its own right; that's like having nothing.

LR: It's impossible, right?

ANTHONY: It's impossible, of course.

LR: So he's saying that you can't make an object out of the subject, the observer cannot be the observed.

ANTHONY: Yes, and this is the same premise as is stated in the Vedanta, that your ultimate consciousness is available for immediate perceptual use but cannot in any way be objectified.[6] It's impossible to objectify your own consciousness.

AH: But he does suggest a way of dealing with it.

ANTHONY: Yes, and that is to identify with your own subjectivity and trace it to its origin.

> IF WE analyse the ego, we find it to be a collection of past memories retained from experience and future hopes or fears which anticipate experience. If we try to seize it, to separate it out by itself, we do not find it to exist in the present moment, only in what has gone and what is to come. In fact, it never really exists in the NOW but only seems to. This means that it is a phantom without substance, a false *idea*.
>
> (v6, 8:2.14 AND *Perspectives*, p. 101)

ANTHONY: The point here is to let you look at the situation in a metaphysical way. If you recall a memory or some experience that you went through or had in the past, and you recognize that it is now only an idea, a memory, a thought— the thing that he's asking you to recognize is that now, while it is happening, it is still just a thought. And if you could transpose that understanding, that all things are thoughts, then the present intense moment is devalued to some extent.

You once had something happen to you and it is now just a thought. You see that the subject was a thought, and what it was experiencing was a thought. In other words, you see that the subject and the object were both included under the notion of thought. Then what makes you think that the very present moment that you're experiencing something is other than thought?

> To DENY himself is to refuse to accept himself as he is at present. It is to become keenly aware that he is spiritually blind, deaf, and dumb and to be intensely eager to gain sight, hearing, and speech. It is to realize that nearly all men complacently mistake this inner paralysis for active existence. . . . (v3, 2:7.1)

ANTHONY: If we say that the ego is one thought followed by another, then each thought would have a fixed content, wouldn't it?

LR: Yes.

ANTHONY: Then that fixed content would be paralyzed. In other words if you take a film and you project it on a screen, the content of one frame or "still" is fixed. And think of that one frame as the ego-thought for that instant, and the next instant you have another frame, and there the ego-thought is again fixed and its contents are fixed and then again you have paralysis and inertia. And following one upon the other you have this situation, right? Then what is the active, if that's inertial and paralyzing? What would be the active? Wouldn't it be the light that's illuminating those "stills"?

RC: And the intelligence that's forming it.

ANTHONY: Yes, by light here I mean intelligence.

NH: It seems that if anyone is to stop functioning with an ego, they would also have to stop functioning with a body. Because you have to exist in the moment-to-moment pattern in order to exist in the world.

ANTHONY: You're not being asked to stop functioning in the world, you're just asked to stop identifying with that inertial context. You are being asked not to identify with that context, the content which is fixed.

FD: In other words, you have to try not to appropriate these images. You have to get away from that identification with the images and go back to that unific consciousness.

ANTHONY: Yes, all right. Although whenever you take flowing water out of the brook and put it in the glass, it never seems to be the same water.

LR: I follow the idea of not living out something in the past or not anticipating the future, which is to say, just apprehend the present at any given moment. But the question still remains, following that same thread, how is it possible to apprehend a content without in some way fixing it?

ANTHONY: Well, I'm pointing out that the fixed content is exactly what he's speaking about as paralysis. If the I is associated with a fixed content, then you are in a state of paralysis. If the I is not identified with it, then you have a free flow. I'm just trying to understand and explain what he's saying about being in the state of inertia and being in the state of creativity, or free. Freedom.

RG: Take the example of the film projector and each frame of the film is that fixed content. Now, the light of the projector shines through each frame. It seems when each frame takes itself to be the light also, then there is a paralysis and you take yourself to be that fixed content. But if you could take the standpoint of the light, you would see the contents flowing. You could talk within the contents but you would see it, it would be an objective act, it wouldn't be a subjective identification.

ANTHONY: That's good.

NH: Doesn't that identification with the light demand that the individual frame be broken down as well?

RG: No, in a movie film, the individual frames just keep going on. The light shines and the film just keeps going on the screen. It doesn't demand that each frame be broken down. All it means is that the light doesn't take itself to be the frame, but can stand back as the light and watch the film play.

NH: But that frame still exists, and if the frame is the ego then the ego must be continuing.

ANTHONY: The frame is gone. The next instant there's another frame.

RG: And that whole series of thoughts is the ego, and it's the identification of the light with each frame, to create the sense of continuity that gives the identification.

ANTHONY: If the light insists on identifying itself with a content of one of the frames then you've got death. If the light doesn't identify with the contents of any frame it flows smoothly.

LR: I follow it.

ANTHONY: You do? Well, now apply it. This is your doing. This is what you *do*. In the case of you or me, who is it that's identifying with the image that's in your mind now?

AH: In the case of the frames that identified with the light, each individual frame usurps the light for itself. It's easy enough then to talk about a content and someone who identifies with it.

ANTHONY: Yes, and then you also have to talk about a light which is entombed in that frame.

AH: Now describe the process of disidentification, where the light doesn't entomb itself.

ANTHONY: It means to let the images go. Let them fly. Don't hold them.

AH: But what is there of my experience that isn't entombed in that frame?

AS: The light?

RG: That which knows?

ANTHONY: You, YOU! Use the simple word, *you.*

HS: How could the light identify with the frame?

RG: The light does not identify with the frame, the frame takes itself to be the light.

ANTHONY: Thoughts take themselves to be the consciousness.

RG: Consciousness never takes itself to be the thoughts.

ANTHONY: Can you give me an instance?

RG: If it could then it wouldn't be conscious, it would be ignorant.

ANTHONY: If you said the consciousness identified with the thoughts, then you would be saying the Overself is identifying with the ego, these thoughts, and therefore now the Overself is the ego.

LR: Is it possible to be *just* the observer and also to participate?

ANTHONY: Do it and find out. All the great ones have testified to its possibility. We recognize that the exercise is carried on by the ego, in the ego, for the ego. We recognize all that. But the thing is to do it. It's going to be theoretical unless you do it.

LR: So why are we discussing the quote?

ANTHONY: So that I could point that out. [*laughter*]

You'll see that even if you do a simple mantram. After a while it goes on by itself. And you say, "How could that be? I'm not even paying attention to it." You could be observing it and it's going on by itself.

DD: You're saying that as long as you have this light you'll have a presentation of images that are illuminated. You can abolish egoity or an attachment to those images, but you'll have a presentation of images if you have this light.

ANTHONY: That's going on, yes. The recognition that the ego is part of the world's being comes upon you and you stop saying that it doesn't exist.

> LET THEM not waste so many words about or against
> this little ego of ours, decrying its character or denying
> its existence, but try to understand what is really
> happening in its short life. Let them find out what is
> actually being wrought out within and around it. Let
> them recognize that the Governor of the World is
> related to it and that we are steeped in the Divinity
> whether we are aware of it or not.   (v6, 8:1.130)

ANTHONY: That's what we try to see in astrology. If we say that the Governor of the World, the Lord of the World, has organized the World-Image and all the creatures within it, then of course there's a very intimate association between the Lord of the World, the structure of your ego, and what the Lord of the World is trying to accomplish.[7] By combining certain ideas, the Lord of the World is trying to show you something about yourself. You're supposed to try to understand what is going on within you and around you. So if you look at an aspect,[8] you can see something about the way this idea is manifesting *you*. Otherwise, how could you cooperate with the World-Idea, without a knowledge of these things?

Maybe you could also see that insofar as the Lord of the World—or let's say the lords of karma—brings about this fabrication, your ego, for whatever number of years, it must love that very much. In other words, the Governor of the World, who creates what we look upon as the natal chart, must love that very much. It loves it completely, but the ego mistakenly understands that as love for itself.

NG: But the ego thinks the Lord of the World did it for *him*.

ANTHONY: Yes. So, one can see that there's a misunderstanding that's going to take place, that the ego is going to misunderstand this love that the World-Mind has for the World-Idea and appropriate it for its own use. But let's not get stuck there.

Maybe it would be a good idea if we could try to make clearer what we mean when we say "ego," "world," and "consciousness."

Is the ego the body? The body is part of the world, is part of the World-Idea, part of the imaged world. And it's distinct from that world, or distinguished from that world. So we could separate these two in our minds. And then when PB says that resident in the body, or presiding in the body, is this power to think, to be aware, these things would belong to the Soul. So we have three factors we're separating in our experience: a world, the ego, and awareness. Now, they're evidently mixed up, so we have to try to unscramble: What is the ego, What is the world image or the world, and What is the Overself?

Now it's true, if we took away the consciousness from the body, we wouldn't be able to say that that ego is aware of a world or that it could think or move—it wouldn't be able to do that. So we'd have the problem of saying, if we took this awareness and distinguished it from the body or the ego, then what would be the ego? If we took away the consciousness, distinguished it from the body, would that be the ego? Or would that body become the ego if the light or consciousness penetrated into it?

THE PERSONAL EGO of man forms itself out of the impersonal life of the universe like a wave forming itself out of the ocean. It constricts, confines, restricts, and limits that infinite life to a small finite area. The wave does just the same to the water of the ocean. The ego shuts out so much of the power and intelligence contained in the universal being that it seems to belong to an entirely different and utterly inferior order of existence. The wave, too, since it forms itself only on the surface of the water gives no indication in its tiny stature of the tremendous depth and breadth and volume of water beneath it.

Consider that no wave exists by itself or for itself, that all waves are inescapably parts of the visible ocean. In the same way, no individual life can separate itself from the All-Life but is always a part of it in some way or other. Yet the idea of separateness is held by millions. This idea is an illusion. From it springs their direst troubles. The work of the quest is simply this: to free the ego from its self-imposed limitations, to let the wave of conscious being subside and straighten itself out into the waters whence it came. The little wave is thus reconverted into the infinite Overself.   (v6, 8:1.102)

ANTHONY: Try to imagine the earth rotating or going around the sun. And surrounding the earth there's what we refer to as the belt, the dragonic belt, that life which is around the earth, and which we call the soul of the earth, all right? Now let's re-read this quote a little at a time.

The personal ego of man forms itself out of the impersonal life of the universe . . .

ANTHONY: The personal life of the man, like my ego, is formed out of this universal life, which is this life which is all around the earth, the soul of the earth, which the Greeks have a name for.[9]

How do I separate myself out from that universal life? At a

certain moment, let's say, I incarnate. At that moment there are certain aspects, and so on. This structure is what I refer to as the ego. This is what has separated itself out from all of that life and isolated itself, or let's say, has carved out an existence for itself within that total life. If I could be allowed to look at it that way.[10]

> . . . It constricts, confines, restricts, and limits that infinite life to a small finite area . . .

ANTHONY: Isn't that exactly what I do once that identification takes place? No longer am I this tremendous and infinite reservoir of understanding and knowledge which the 360 degrees of the zodiac would represent, but I'm restricted to these things which I picked out, which would be my peculiar tendencies and habits. All you have to do is go to those points in your natal chart, and you see: Those are your habits, those are your tendencies. That's the way you operate, and you cling to that way of operating.

For instance, my Saturn degree says I have to see the practical and I have to see the idealistic, and I have to work with the two of them. But if I cling to that, then I limit myself to looking at everything this way and the consequence is that I become a finite creature. It doesn't matter how great the idea may be, even if I operate with it archetypally, I still have made myself into a finite creature.

> . . . The wave does just the same to the water of the ocean. The ego shuts out so much of the power and intelligence contained in the universal being that it seems to belong to an entirely different and utterly inferior order of existence . . .

ANTHONY: Of course, we could see that when we make a

comparison between the sage and an ordinary person. It's like the ordinary person belongs to an entirely different order of being—or we could say that the sage belongs to an entirely different type.

The sage would be the one to whom all this is accessible—he's open to it. Not that karma will determine that, but that the Ideas are open to him. He's open inwardly, and what he has to deal with, or what he has to give forth, he will.

MB: I think that so far the quote is talking about the ego as being the same in substance with the universal being—is that right?

ANTHONY: Yes, yes.

MB: But could you say that there is more than just substance involved here? We're talking about universal being that has qualities.

ANTHONY: Yes. But by qualities, you mean Ideas. The same as the Moslems and Plotinus—as soon as you say "qualities" you're speaking about Ideas. Otherwise you're speaking about nothing. I wouldn't be able to understand what you're talking about. So as soon as you bring in the Ideas, what we're saying is that this universal being has substance. What is its substance? All those Ideas. And we have pointed out over and over again that the usage of the term "substance" is not in the sense of "matter," but "ideational consciousness," something like that. Like we think of the wisdom of God or the Ideas of God, and we could think of them as a substance, pure substance, pure being. *This* is not substance [*knocks on a wooden pillar*]. This is illusion.

MB: So we're saying that the ego participates . . .

ANTHONY: . . . in that universal substance . . .

MB: . . . . in those Ideas, but in an illusive sort of way.

ANTHONY: Yes. And if you introspect into your behavior, if you watch the way you operate, you'll see that those are the degrees in your natal chart.

Those are habits. But, of course, I think you got the point that has to be realized: These habits are *derived* from the great archetypal Ideas, that is, from this pure substance or this universal being of the earth, the earth's life. But now you have to let go of the fixity that these habits operate with in you. Thinking that you always have to do it this fixed way is a mistake on your part.

NG: How would you train yourself? Can you really train yourself?

ANTHONY: Well, you noticed when you were with PB— was there anything fixed about his behavior? From moment to moment he kept you jumping and hopping. You couldn't figure out what the next moment would be, because it was so spontaneous. He wasn't operating with any of these fixed ways—you know, that you could say, "That's the way PB works." When you were with him, you couldn't anticipate his next move. Whereas I can anticipate your next move because I know what your habits are like.

That's what astrology is largely based on—the fact that our habits are so strong that the astrologer could depend on them to guarantee their performance. Let's read a little more.

... The wave, too, since it forms itself only on the surface of the water gives no indication in its tiny stature of the tremendous depth and breadth and volume of water beneath it ...

ANTHONY: Now, do you have some clue? I would try to put it this way: You have some indication of the nature of this vast subconscious which is operating within you. In other words, all those degrees of the zodiac—that's your subconscious. And that's included in your makeup. But you restrict yourself. You say, "No, I'm only these ten[11]—I don't know any of that other stuff." Remember how often you people would deny the fact that the I did it, and you'd say, "It's not my I that did it, it's someone else's I—it's the Witness I that did it."

RC: So you call those natal planets the conscious ego because through them you can impose some sort of structure on the consciousness that flows through.

ANTHONY: Yes—that universal substance—yes. Now, the other interesting thing about that structure is that it's *self-formulating*. It goes on recuperating and reformulating itself over and over again, from incarnation to incarnation, too, let alone within one life.

You could think of all the Ideas and the planetary functioning, and the meaning of these two together in their operation would be the result of what we call the subconscious. Subconscious is just a word; I have to understand what you mean by it, and not assume what you mean.

. . . Consider that no wave exists by itself or for itself . . .

ANTHONY: Can you see that astrologically? There can't be any of that selection by itself. And the waves are constantly being made. The transits never stop, so there's waves being constantly made.[12] Don't worry—they'll never come to an end. You remember Mahler and Brahms on the bridge, and Brahms says, "There are no more great melodies," and Mahler says, "Look, there's the last wave!" [*laughter*] Insofar as these transits are going on, these creations of ego will be taking place. Go on.

. . . Consider that no wave exists by itself or for itself,
that all waves are inescapably parts of the visible ocean.
In the same way, no individual life can separate itself
from the All-Life but is always a part of it in some way
or other . . .

ANTHONY: So if we think of this formulation that's taking place, then we could think of the earth's undivided mind, the whole of the solar system, as this infinite life that is constantly organizing these points or centers of consciousness that we're going to call the ego. And they cannot be separated from the infinite life, but the ego will do that. And insofar as it does, it immediately cuts itself off from that.

Once I start believing in my ego as the reality, I've given up any belief in the higher power. But don't take the inverse. Don't say "I don't believe in my ego," and therefore you think that you believe in the higher power. [*laughter*] Wait until you find out if you really believe in it. And you find out maybe you don't believe in it, but it was just in your imagination. So you have to wait for the finding out whether you really believe in it.

. . . Yet the idea of separateness is held by millions. This
idea is an illusion. From it springs their direst troubles.
The work of the quest is simply this: to free the ego
from its self-imposed limitations, to let the wave of
conscious being subside and straighten itself out into
the waters whence it came. The little wave is thus
reconverted into the infinite Overself.

JL: Sometimes I think that the nature principle is great enough to provide complete sustenance for the ego.

ANTHONY: Do you mean by nature principle the universal substance or universal life of the earth?

JL: Yes.

ANTHONY: Wouldn't you think it's great enough to provide a *vehicle* that the soul could inhabit?

JL: Would an ego that is fully developed have its limitations then?

ANTHONY: Naturally, the limitations would be the body

you have and the ego that came along with that, that has taken possession of that body. But they're not fixed limitations—they could be overcome.

The important thing in the discussion here is to recognize that the subconscious is all these degrees, and the functioning of these degrees produces individual animal bodies, and these animal bodies are a storehouse. The degrees represent or symbolize all these Ideas inherent in the body of a person, and a tremendous wisdom-knowledge goes into making the body of a person.

Now, if you take it from there, we'd have to speak about a consciousness coming into that and taking possession of it. So I'm still trying to get to the fundamental thing—the ego, the world, and the consciousness—so that I could understand something of the nature of the ego. When the consciousness permeates that body, then an ego and a world arise at the same time. Now I have to try to understand, "Well, what do I mean when I say ego and what do I mean when I say consciousness?" The world isn't aware of itself. The ego can't be aware of itself. That which is aware of the ego is not the ego. So I have to separate these things for my own understanding to get a better picture of what I'm talking about.

The ego is very slippery—the profoundest depths of pleasure and pain are there. It goes all the way up to the top with us. Anyone who doesn't know about the ego is not on the quest; he's on a TV journey.

THE TRUE self of man is hidden in a central core of stillness, a central vacuum of silence. This core, this vacuum occupies only a pinpoint in dimension. All around it there is a ring of thoughts and desires constituting the imagined self, the ego. This ring is constantly fermenting with fresh thoughts, constantly changing with fresh desires, and alternately bubbling with joy or heaving with grief. Whereas the centre is forever at rest, the ring around it is never at rest; whereas the centre bestows peace, the ring destroys it.

(v6, 8:1.32 AND *Perspectives*, p. 103)

RC: The quote seems to be discussing the process of thinking about what's involved in the consciousness producing this ring of thoughts, rather than two unrelated terms.

ANTHONY: You know that they're not unrelated for me. When I speak about consciousness I'm speaking about the whole cosmic circuit;[13] and when I'm speaking about thought I'm speaking about the production of that cosmic circuit through the intermediary of aspects and so on—all that, which is a very organized and highly determined knowledge-wisdom.

You have to understand what the nature of this individual existence is, because it is the cause of all our misery, and yet strangely enough, it is dearer to us than anything we can think of. So, evidently, there must be a lot of value in our suffering.

We said that in order for there to be an individual existence we had to think of this infinite light or this mind which is boundless—we can't speak about it, except in this sense of being authentic being. And only when this is associated with, or permeates a cluster of thought, can you speak about an individual existent. And then I went further and gave the example: Now I examine into my behavior, into my thinking, and every time I have a thought, I can see that that thought is a manifestation of the degrees I'm working with.

For instance, I keep pounding a thought, I get a solution to something, I'm not satisfied. I keep trying to understand it more deeply and I keep doing that. You can see that that's one of the tendencies in my chart, right? You look at my Mercury degree and you say, "He's got to get to the bottom of something." You see that's a tendency. Well, is that tendency the core, the reality of my being? No. My being permeates all that, or let's say, has wrapped itself around that. But it takes these two mixed together, my being and the degrees/planets, to produce the entity you know as Anthony.

> THE UNIQUENESS of each person, his difference from every other person, may be metaphysically explained as due to the effort of Infinite Mind to express itself infinitely within the finite limitation of time and space, form and appearance.   (v16, 25:1.157)

ANTHONY: Every type and variety of person that could be expressed by the planetary functioning will so be expressed. Each one would be unique. If you think of every person ever born, look at the peculiarity and uniqueness of his or her natal chart: This infinite variety expresses the World-Mind. You could put it that way. Every possible type is going to be expressed.

> EACH HUMAN being has a specific work to do—to express the uniqueness that is himself. It can be delegated to no one else. In doing it, if he uses the opportunity aright, he may be led to the great Uniqueness which is superpersonal, beyond his ego and behind all egos.
>   (v2, 1:5.19)

ANTHONY: There's a very positive statement about your ego. If you refer to the natal chart, that's your very particular uniqueness. It's yours and no one else's. There are no two alike. Each and every person is a very special and unique interpretation or manifestation of his or her own higher self. So there are no two egos that are alike.

Then he points out that there's a special work delegated to that person. The Hindus would call that your *dharma*. Whatever it is—whether it's to be a warrior or an insurance salesman or whatever—that's your particular *dharma*. And if you do that faithfully and correctly, it could lead you to the reality which is behind your ego as well as to the reality which is behind every ego.

Uniqueness here doesn't refer to the fact that you have to be a certain kind of tradesman or merchant. It refers to something that has to be worked out in you. We try to understand that in terms of the chart, the particular ideas that you're working out. That's your special uniqueness. You must express it and that means working in the world, and doing whatever it is you have to do. And generally you'll have to do it.

AH: Is it possible *not* to express them?

ANTHONY: Yes, it's possible. A person can deviate, yes.

AH: There's some psychological deformity?

ANTHONY: It could be that. It could be circumstance. It could be many reasons. But generally the tendency is for us to follow through what our uniqueness is because there's a compelling reason that's operating, through which we feel that this is the way we best are. That's usually your destiny: the living out of the ideas that you embody, the special uniqueness that you are. We could leave out the reactions to it—that's the way you spoil it.

LG: The chart provides a selection of the total possibilities available to a person. Can there be growth to a point where there is a freedom from those particulars, a freedom from the ego? Can you speak about an ability to use all those possibilities? Would all the 360 degrees be available to a sage?

ANTHONY: Yes, the sage is much more sensitive to *all* the ideas than an individual who is compelled and organized by a structure of particular ideas.

LG: Those 360 degrees constitute everyone's chart although there is a specification for each person.

ANTHONY: They constitute everyone's chart? You mean they're the content? But each one sees them quite differently from everyone else, because everyone is very particularized. We're just using the chart as an example, a mathematical example, that there can't be two alike. That means that you are very, very special, and so am I.

LG: Well, they're identified with that ego structure.

ANTHONY: They're not *identified* with that ego structure. They *are* that ego. They are that structure. So it is through that structure that you see all the ideas, which means that your version of all the ideas will be different from someone else's version of all the ideas. The uniqueness refers to the relationships among the planets and everything else, if you are to speak of this particular individual and no one else.

RG: That's the little uniqueness. There are two uniquenesses.

ANTHONY: Yes, that's the little uniqueness. The great Uniqueness is the intelligible world in each and every soul.

FD: Take a lot of great artists, each expresses something unique. Their life was a work of art in a lot of ways. There is a uniqueness. They have been brought to a degree of realization.

ANTHONY: There is special uniqueness that an individual lives, and the closer it conforms to the World-Idea, the closer it conforms to the great Uniqueness. Your ego is part of the World-Idea. As it evolves it will conform more and not less to the World-Idea. Eventually you'll be pushed right into the World-Idea and be like part and parcel of the World-Idea. Then you are the great Uniqueness. When you stop seeing yourself as a personality, distinct and separate from everyone else, and you can see that also from within the realm of the whole of the impersonal, then you are at the level of the great Uniqueness.

THE KNOWLEDGE that no two human beings are alike refers to their bodies and minds. But this leaves out the part of their nature which is spiritual, which is found and experienced in deep meditation. In that, the deepest part of their conscious being, the personal self vanishes; only consciousness-in-itself, thought-free, world-free, remains. This is the source of the "I" feeling, and it is exactly alike in the experience of all other human beings. This is the part which never dies, "where God and man may mingle."   (v14, 22:3.380)

ANTHONY: Please read it again, one part at a time.

The knowledge that no two human beings are alike refers to their bodies and minds. . . .

ANTHONY: How about that? Would the natal chart prove that?

TS: Yes. The basic meaning of the natal chart is that it is the mind-body complex or the ideas, the reason principles, which constitute the mind and the body.

ME: When you're using the word "mind" here, what do you mean?

LR: Psyche?

VM: How about if you use mind as the collection and functioning and relationship of all those reason principles which are delineated in the astrological chart?

ANTHONY: Good. That would be good. That would be what we refer to as the "psyche."

. . . But this leaves out the part of their nature which is spiritual, which is found and experienced in deep meditation . . .

ANTHONY: The stillness, that quietness in you, that would be the spiritual part. Pure consciousness, if you want to call it that.

TS: How would you relate that to the idea of the undivided mind, or the cosmic circuit?

ANTHONY: Well, that would be the next step, because the stillness in itself is not enough. It leads you to the spiritual part of yourself, or to the undivided mind.

> ... In that, the deepest part of their conscious being, the personal self vanishes; only consciousness-in-itself, thought-free, world-free, remains ...

ANTHONY: In that state, thought-free, being free of the world thought, I cannot claim that this is a state I enjoy in common with others or that it is singular. All such qualifications are meaningless.

RG: Because there's nobody there to make the qualifications.

ANTHONY: Yes. There's no personal I. You know that fellow we were talking about, who has to see the practical and the theoretical together, who has to burrow down, who has to complain about this? That person isn't there, so he can't make any of these statements that we want to make. Go ahead.

> ... This is the source of the "I" feeling, and it is exactly alike in the experience of all other human beings. This is the part which never dies, "where God and man may mingle."

ANTHONY: Basically, what he's saying is that this is where we'll all agree. There would be unanimity about the experiencing. But we won't agree about the way we understand the World-Idea. Each one will come up with a slightly different interpretation, because each has to operate through the uniqueness of his personality. But in that realm, we'll agree. So we're brothers in Christ, but cross swords down here.

How CAN man fully express himself unless he fully develops himself? The spiritual evolution which requires him to abandon the ego runs parallel to the mental evolution which requires him to perfect it. (v6, 8:1.158)

ANTHONY: We said that the structure of the planets at the moment of birth represents the ego. Now the rational soul[14] is always going around that and it's trying to make necessary additions, subtractions—whatever's necessary to perfect the ego. That's part of the mental perfection that he's speaking about. The ego is being built up. It's being developed to the ultimate degree possible by the rational soul.

PC: Would you include the rational soul itself within the ego?

ANTHONY: No, that's *correcting* the ego. So it would be the rational soul, that would be the *mental*, trying to correct the categories of the imagination. But then the *spiritual* would be the super-rational soul[15] also coming in and trying to bring its light into the ego. But, strangely enough, he says that when the superior consciousness comes into the ego structure it gets appropriated by the ego and then the ego considers it as its own functioning. That's where the ego is very cunning. So a big idea comes into you, and you say, "I got an idea." No. You were given the idea; you didn't have it.

Let me try this way. At the moment of birth, there's a fixed relationship among the planets which reveals something about that ego. The first thing we have to recognize is that there is a kind of universal life surrounding the world—we call it the dragon—and that your life is a particle from that universal life. Now, in itself, that's the ego. But when the series

of thoughts or the ego says, "This is *my* life," it has appropriated, separated itself from that. Now it is the fixed ego
structure, fixed in the sense that the possibilities are fixed.
That is, you're not going to think about just anything but
you're going to think along certain lines. The natal aspects
show the way that's going to manifest.

This is very important. There's a universal life system that
pervades the earth, and at the moment of birth you are, so to
speak, separated out. We should really say we're distinguished,
not separate, from that universal life; but the ego says,
"No, I'm different from everyone else." That's the separation.
So everything that takes place within the functioning of the
natal planets and the aspects they have, is within the ego.

RG: But it still seems that the appropriation of that structure as yours is different than the structure itself. The appropriation has to be extrinsic to the structure itself.

ANTHONY: No. That this is *my* life is a false assumption
inherent in that structure, in the very thought-processes that
it generates. The notion that you as an ego are separate from
everyone else is inherent in that very way of functioning, not
something imposed upon you by the universal life.

RG: How do you get out of the fact that the appropriation
is inherent in the thing?

ANTHONY: How do you get out of it? The way you get free
of the identification would be the accumulating and climactic
effect that the rational soul has on the ego and that the super-
rational soul has on the ego. That's the way you'd ultimately
get out of it.

RG: And there's a transformation that brings a realization
that in fact the ego structure is part of the universal life and is
not separate from it.

ANTHONY: Yes. In other words, the ego's becoming rational—or let's say it's assimilating rationality. Only as fixed in
the aspectual relationships at the moment of birth, is it to be
considered the ego.

RG: Is it utterly necessary that the person identify with these fixed modes?

ANTHONY: As long as he's operating within the natal structure he's going to say, "That's me. That's mine."

RG: Right , but when he gets out of that he'll see that it isn't.

ANTHONY: Yes.

RG: But it's a funny paradox, because those same natal planets then become not that identified ego, but rational.

ANTHONY: No, it still remains the ego of that soul. It remains the field within which that soul will manifest and develop the potentialities that are in that ego.

RG: But the person doesn't seem to take it as "mine" at that point.

ANTHONY: Have you noticed that? Your development usually means you have to forget the "mine." You can't be thinking "I'm doing this" when you're doing something.

RG: Are you also saying that while the ego basically equals the planets in the natal chart when operating as the categories of the imagination, nonetheless, when the transiting planets operate as the rational soul powers, that's not the ego?

ANTHONY: That's the rational soul. And you can see the mental development that is being forced upon the ego by the rational soul constantly, without interruption. The development and the refinement of the ego is taking place because you're constantly having transits going on. That's the development by the rational soul. But the other thing we're talking about is that when the higher knowing comes into the person there's an appropriation of that higher knowing by the ego. The reason I'm emphasizing this is to show how the ego can take over the higher knowledge and insist that it is *its* knowledge, and it is *its* being, that *it* is spiritual. That's the whole point.

RG: The *it* arises through the categories of the imagination, not through the rational soul powers. That's the . . .

ANTHONY: . . . egoism.

RC: The egoism! *That's* the distinction you're making between the natal and the transiting planets. Now wouldn't the ideal be that when the rational soul powers transit, they would make the natal chart rational also? Aren't we allowing for that possibility, too?

ANTHONY: Exactly. That's what he spoke about when he spoke about the need to perfect the ego and develop it. Whereas the spiritual evolution would be implemented through the outer three planets—which require *abandoning* the ego—the rational souls from Saturn inward are demanding that the ego gets *fulfilled.*

RC: And the extent to which the *abandonment* gets accomplished has a lot to do with the extent to which the *fulfillment* will be accomplished. The more impartial you can be towards your own ego, the more you can look at yourself as if you were somebody else and see how you measure up to your own inner standards, the more capable you'll be of perfecting it. But if you're stuck inside of it, then it becomes you! In fact, you don't have to do anything in it.

ANTHONY: Isn't that what we try to do when we make a dossier or a brief portrait of the planets in a person's chart? What I'm really asking is try to make a dossier, a thumbnail picture in your mind of the way this ego is organized and the way it functions because of the basic organization that it's operating with. Once we get that, then we could see how the transits are affecting it. So when we were studying Emerson, for example, and we were putting together some of the ego structure of that person, we began to see that there's something really worthwhile built into the structure of the ego— if we know what to do, instead of deriding it, kicking it out, saying it doesn't exist, it's illusory.

AH: The parallel evolution of this ego and the spiritual, do they work in unison in some way?

ANTHONY: Yes.

AH: But they also are in conflict continually.

ANTHONY: No, they're not in conflict. When someone is approaching a spiritual level of integrity, you'll always find they are very humble and simple. As an individual is getting perfected mentally, there's a spiritual distance from that ego that's being evolved. There's no conflict there.

AH: So this is the development of the ego in the context of a spiritual path. It's not the development of the ego in the context of genius.

ANTHONY: That would be included also. A person is developing all the potentials that are within their ego. Let's take a Michelangelo or a Da Vinci, all right? There's inherent in the very structure of the personality this potentiality for genius and he develops it. But if he starts saying, "Ain't I the greatest?" then he's egotistical. This you don't need.

AH: We develop that which prevents us from our spiritual birthright?

ANTHONY: The development of the ego and spiritual freedom from it: What else could you develop?

AB: The mental development of the ego still goes on, but the attachment to it or the appropriation of it is what's given up in the spiritual.

AH: Well, then the conclusion would be that the mental development is not, after all, in conflict with the spiritual development.

ANTHONY: Exactly. That's one of the things we've been hammering away at for a long time. When certain organizations insist, for example, that you do not listen to music, you do not have art, this that and the other, I think they're unspiritual.

HS: Mental development isn't necessarily spiritual.

ANTHONY: It's true that a mentally developed person doesn't have to become spiritual, but it's pretty hard for a

person to become spiritual without a certain mental development.

RC: In the spiritual person, the whole ego process is objective as an activity of the universal life force.

HS: Could you say why you equate objectivity with spirituality here?

ANTHONY: Your ego becomes more objective to you the
closer you're identified with the higher consciousness.

AH: Is that to say that perfection of this ego is actually
when the ego becomes more and more spiritual?

ANTHONY: No. We made a distinction. The mental development of the ego is one thing. The spirituality is another.
And they are parallel processes. As the ego is developing, there
could be a detachment from that development and yet that
development could go on.

AH: But that development of the ego is in no sense a spiritual one.

ANTHONY: It very well can be or it may not be. We have
met people of extreme intellectual ability who use it for other
purposes than spiritual ones.

HS: So when you want to analyze, and you say, "I would
like to spiritualize my existence," what does that mean? A
planet goes on a degree in relation to your natal chart: What
are you saying about that?

RC: Something that has normally been presented to you in
a dualistic bifurcated mode, with a subject set up in contra-
distinction to an object, might be able to become available to
you as a universal truth in which it's appreciated by a kind of
consciousness that doesn't operate in that bifurcated mode.

ANTHONY: The point is that at that moment you will objectively perceive the way your ego functions. A perception
of that nature automatically calls into operation the higher
consciousness. You perceive objectively the way your ego
functions.

HS: I think there's made available a conceptual mode to think about it.

ANTHONY: All right, let's even say in a conceptual mode, that's good. And in a conceptual mode, you perceive the way your ego is functioning. Before you couldn't see it at all but now conceptually you can perceive the way your ego functions. *That's a spiritual effort* because it has detached you from the identification with the ego and put it at a distance. Even if it's only a few inches away.

HS: Is there any point where you abandon the conceptual mode and think about the existence directly?

ANTHONY: But *you* have the idea that this is some kind of conceptual knowledge! And I'm trying to point out that it isn't. At the moment you perceive the way your ego functions, that moment is *not* conceptual knowledge. It's real knowledge, not the highest but good. You saw that at that moment that wasn't you. At that moment, you had an instance of higher knowledge. Why do you insist on denying it?

HS: You say the moment you perceive the way that ego functions is good knowledge. Now the relationship to natal planets on the degrees . . . ?

ANTHONY: That's subjective functioning, the way the ego functions.

HS: And the mode of seeing the way the ego functions?

ANTHONY: That's modeless. You say you see it. You're not using words to see it. You have this bugaboo that conceptual knowledge is always something that's operative, that you can't see with concepts, that in order for me to see a snake I have to bring into my brain the word "snake" and then I see it.

HS: I thought in order to see a snake you just look at the snake. The snake is right in front of you.

ANTHONY: Exactly. The moment that you see the way your ego subjectively functions, at that moment you have spiritual knowledge. I'm not saying you're *Brahman*, all right?

I'm just saying you have spiritual knowledge at that moment. It's the most elementary tenet of almost any psychology—if they expect abreaction to operate. They want you to *see.*

HS: To see from the outside.

ANTHONY: Well, you can't see from the inside. It's not the manipulation of content within the ego, but getting outside it.

AH: How do you tell the difference?

ANTHONY: You will know that it is so because it's efficacious right then and there.

HS: Efficacious in that it's freeing, detaching?

ANTHONY: Yes. It's not counterfeit. It's quite beneficial. It may not be a big *satori* that will blow your head off, but really this does have value.

RC: I read about someone who was trying to break a cannon, and he hit it with a hammer hundreds of times. Finally the cannon broke and people asked him which blow broke it and he said, "All of them."

ANTHONY: Did you get the point of the joke? It takes a long time to get illuminated. And it's going to take a series of blows, a series of insights, maybe a few lifetimes of insights.

HS: Wang Yang-Ming says it takes a hundred deaths and a thousand trials.

ANTHONY: We'll have to expand that a little bit: a thousand lives and a million trials, the way we are going! [*laughter*] These are such obvious truths; all they require is a momentary disassociation. All they require is attention, that's all they require. We hope to satisfy you before we are finished. YOU, not your ego.

NOTES

1. See also pages 148-153 in this chapter.

2. See *Looking into Mind* by Anthony Damiani (Larson Publications, Burdett, NY, 1990) for more on this tradition.

3. In Buddhism, the "*nidana* chain" is a nexus of twelve mutually related causes that power the "wheel of life and death," or "wheel of cyclic existence." Of these twelve links of combined, dependent origination, "ignorance" is the first.

4. The tales of Gautama Buddha's previous lives.

5. Thought can only do this when suffused and taken possession of by the "light" emanating from the Soul. Two points are essential here. First, the light spoken of is not the Soul itself but rather an emanent from the Soul. Second, it is only as part of this "conjoining" of light and thought that thought can mis-take itself as the subject. The latter is the "mistaken thinking" referred to earlier.

6. See Citsuka's *Tattva Pradipika*. The specific reference also appears on page 140 of T.M.P. Mahadevan's book, *The Philosophy of Advaita*, Ganesh & Co., Madras, India, 1969.

7. That each individual's mental and spiritual development is part of the cosmos' own evolution is an essential feature of PB's writings on the ego. The remainder of this chapter briefly outlines a creative and remarkably fertile approach Anthony used to illustrate this key point. While readers unsympathetic to the symbolism introduced here may move on to chapter four, those willing to experiment with it may find it a highly valuable tool. A more complete development of this approach, with specific applications, will appear in a subsequent book devoted exclusively to that purpose.

8. Astrological "aspects" arise when planets stand in significant

geometric relationship to one another or to other key points in an individual's natal chart. They indicate meaningful combinations of the ideas represented by the 360 degrees of the symbolic zodiac, and are derived from the geometry of the mandala (in the East) or from Pythagorean symbolism (in the West). See also chapter two, note 6.

9. Plotinus speaks of "the being known as Hestia (Earth-Mind) and Demeter (Earth-Soul)—a nomenclature indicating the human evolution of these truths." See *Ennead* IV.4.27, MacKenna translation.

10. From the geocentric viewpoint, each of the planets represents a certain soul power operating within the conditions of the earth sphere in which we live. At the moment of an individual's birth, each planet occupies a specific degree in the geocentric zodiac. These positions constitute the individual's natal chart, his or her unique "matrix of thoughts."

Despite the fact that the planets themselves move onward immediately, the tendencies symbolized in the natal positions persist as dominant influences on the way that person will create and experience his or her image of the world. As unfolding that image in terms of their natal aspects, the planets are symbols of the soul or psychological functions such as evaluation, communication, etc. Anthony later uses the term "categories of the imagination" for their operation at this level.

11. The degrees the ten planets occupied at the moment of birth.

12. As the planets continue to move through the zodiac, they form new aspects to the natal positions (i.e., to the positions they occupied at the moment of birth). These motions, and the new combinations of ideas they represent, are called "transits" to the natal structure.

13. "Cosmic circuit" here means the infinite life organizing centers of consciousness as spoken of on page 165.

14. The reasoning phase of the soul, as first mentioned on pp. 112-113. Anthony symbolizes this phase of the soul as the motions of the planets visible to the naked eye from earth, i.e., those from Saturn inward, including the sun and moon.

15. Anthony is applying the classical Platonic notion of three levels of soul: 1) embodied soul, operating as the categories of the imagination; 2) rational or reasoning soul, which Plotinus in *Ennead* i.i.13 calls the "characteristic Act of our Soul," and 3) super-rational soul, the phase of soul that is directly informed by the divine Ideas.

The latter phase is beyond reason and delivers the presence of the Ideas as transcending the cosmic activity. Anthony symbolizes its operation in us as the motions of the outer three planets, Uranus, Neptune, and Pluto. These three, though not visible from earth to the unaided eye, were integral to Egyptian, Chinese, Greek, and Hindu traditional cosmogony.

No ONE ELSE can do for a man what Nature is tutoring him to do for himself, that is, to surrender the ego to the higher self. Without such surrender no man can attain the consciousness of that higher self. It is useless to look to a master to make for him this tremendous change-over within himself. No master could do it. The proper way and the only way is to give up this pathetic clinging to his own power, to his own littleness, and to his own limitations. To turn so completely against himself demands from a man an extreme emotional effort of the rarest kind and also of the most painful kind. For to surrender the ego is to crucify it.

(v6, 8:4.211)

WE WHO honour philosophy so highly cannot afford to be other than honest with ourselves. We have to acknowledge that the end of all our striving is surrender. No human being can do other than this—an utterly humble prostration, where we dissolve, lose the ego, lose ourselves— the rest is paradox and mystery.

(v13, 20:5.11)

CHAPTER FOUR

UNITING WITH
THE SOURCE

WHEN THE inner history of the human entity is known
and its lessons absorbed, the problem offers itself: "How
can I escape from myself?" The answer will necessarily
show that the ego can succeed only to a certain degree
in such a venture, but it not only cannot go beyond this
but will not even try to do so. How can it consent to its
own death?   (v6, 8:4.433)

KD: Anthony, would you mind commenting on the first part?
For me everything centers around the line: "When the inner
history of the human entity is known and its lessons absorbed,
the problem offers itself." It sounds like this is something
that happens, a life process where at a certain stage of development the problem arises and then the answer is given. Is
that just something that happens after the living of life, that
there's a recognition that I'm the cause of the circumstances
that I find myself in—a recognition of the truth of karma?

ANTHONY: Maybe I could rephrase it, just say it in different words. How can the "I," which is a self-actualizing process, undo itself? And if I try to undo myself, isn't that more
doing, and doesn't that strengthen the ego? Consequently:
Catch-22. I'm in a double-bind.

KD: When you say "self-actualizing" you mean . . .

ANTHONY: From instant to instant, this "I" is constantly recreating itself and maintaining itself. So again, parenthetically speaking now, if I am in this self-actualizing process and wish to undo it, wish to stop it, cancel it out, anything I do will strengthen that very process. Consequently, I'm in a double-bind.

KD: Does that perception come at a certain stage?

ANTHONY: It will happen to a person who has reached some maturity. It won't happen to a primitive; he won't be concerned about that.

You must try to remember—and this is very important— that the "I" is constantly, incessantly actualizing itself, every moment of time. You have to keep that in mind, because that's what the "I" is. The "I" is this *process*. It's like mental combustion. It feeds on itself, supplies the fuel and feeds on itself. Keep that in mind.

This is what you are. Now, how do you stop this? If you try to stop it, you have to make an effort. If you make an effort, the ego is getting stronger. If the ego's getting stronger, then how can you undo what you are? So it's a double-bind. You can't get out of it.

Oh, you might improve things a little bit. Instead of being a big cheat, you become a small cheat and then less of a cheat; then finally you become a little honest and become more honest, more and more honest. But the fact still remains that the ego is this process which—any time it attempts to stop itself or undo itself—feeds itself, gets stronger.

MB: Is the arisal of that question an important landmark?

ANTHONY: You will never forget it when it happens.

HS: And the formulation of the question, is that the ego within itself?

ANTHONY: Yes. The ego is coming to this recognition of its own nature.

HS: And it could be an actual formulation?

ANTHONY: Oh, yes. You could actually get to a position where you say, "I hate you!" And I don't mean "hate" in the sense of love and hate, in the sense of opposites. I don't mean hate in that sense. I mean the recognition of what it is, that it is this process.

HS: I read a quote in Gurdjieff that said, "Anything that belongs to it, dislike."

ANTHONY: Again, won't that strengthen the ego? Every time the ego likes something, and I make up my mind to dislike it because the ego likes it, the ego is getting stronger.

HS: Wouldn't you say that at some point there's a certain self-revulsion?

ANTHONY: Oh, yes. The Buddhists are very fond of that word. There arises self-revulsion.

HS: Could you say "hate"?

ANTHONY: No, self-revulsion I think would be more accurate, because hate will always bring up its opposite. And this is *not* in the realm of the opposites. It's an inner recognition. The fruit recognizes that it's rotten. It's a natural process in the sense that after satiation with experience the ego can come to the recognition that all this leads to vanity. That's all it ends up in. So it can end up as a process of recognizing that the very nature of the ego *is* what it is.

KD: And that's the lesson that is absorbed?

ANTHONY: That's how you come to that recognition— from all the lessons you absorb. But I think the essential point in this quote is the recognition that you're in a double-bind, because when that revulsion occurs and you want to do something about it, you'll see that anything you do about it just reinforces it, makes it stronger. Just like when you sit down and say, "I'm going to meditate very hard," you've already spoiled it because "I'm going to meditate very hard" shows the ego's in there, and it's going to do its best to remain there.

AH: You can't do anything about it because any *doing* is a reinforcement.

ANTHONY: If you *do* anything about it, the doer gets bigger.

AH: But to not-do is also a reinforcement?

ANTHONY: That's reinforcement too, sure. A double-bind.

AH: Then I can't even ask the question: "Well, what do you do?" [*laughter*]

ANTHONY: You take a deep breath.

But basically until the higher power comes along and helps you, you're going to be caught there. You're going to be in a state of neither here nor there. There isn't very much you *can* do. But some circumstances may come along and help you separate more from the ego.

PC: Wouldn't the process of recognizing that and observing it bring about a change in itself?

ANTHONY: First of all, it's not a process of recognition, like I tried to point out in the metaphor that the fruit is rotten. It's being. This is the fruit. This is it; it's rotten. The ego comes to that kind of inward understanding, whereas "recognition" will make us think of something objective, out there, something that I'm going to know. It's intrinsic in the very process of the ego's maturation to reach that stage where it recognizes, in this way, what its nature is.

PC: We're talking about this kind of direct observation that has to take place.

ANTHONY: Basically, that's what the revulsion is. That *is* direct observation. Revulsion isn't something you know as "out there." When we say that the fruit is rotten, we're saying that the ego has this intrinsic self-recognition of its own nature. Because the ego will always set about trying to *do* something: "Well, now that I understand the situation, I'm going to go ahead and do something about it." So it'll bring about some disciplines or some more tricks or exercises, but it won't get out of the *cul de sac* that it's in. That's the important thing to understand about this situation.

cs: During that time, couldn't you pray?

ANTHONY: Oh, you could always pray, always pray, but I would be inclined to think that once revulsion takes place, *it* is a prayer, in a sense.

AH: There's one quote where PB says the mark of an old soul is that it prefers non-existence in balance with existence.

ANTHONY: The mark of an old soul is when you've been clubbed enough times over the head that you've had it. "No more." You don't want any more.

AH: That's what PB means by the equal desire for non-existence?

ANTHONY: When the desire not to reincarnate any more gets as strong as the desire to constantly experience, when that happens, now you're ready for the quest.

> WHEN THE wish for non-existence becomes as continuous as the thirst for repeated earthly existence formerly was, when with George Darley, the early nineteenth-century English poet, he can say, "There to lay me down at peace / In my own first nothingness," he has become an old soul.
>
> (v6, 8:4.358)

ANTHONY: What would "my own first nothingness" be?

AH: My Overself.

ANTHONY: Yes, before the tendencies started.

HS: And this desire for non-existence?

ANTHONY: You don't want to be reborn anymore. You've had enough. And this gets you going on the path. A young soul for whom the world and the manifestation of the world have all this glamour is not going to be like that. He's not going to feel that he's had enough of the world.

AH: The Tibetans make quite an issue of generating the desire to leave cyclic existence.

ANTHONY: Yes, but if you didn't have enough lives, you

may not be able to generate that desire to leave cyclic existence. You may generate the desire that you want to keep
coming back, as many lives as possible.

HS: And this desire arises in the ego?

ANTHONY: Yes, all desires will ultimately trace back to
the ego.

HS: And this desire to leave cyclic existence is an appropriate desire for the quest?

ANTHONY: Oh yes.

HS: So from within the ego itself there could arise the
proper desire?

ANTHONY: Well, I don't know if I would put it that way. I
would put it this way. This ego that you're talking about suffered so much that it's ready to put aside the desire to go on
existing. The residue of all that suffering will be a counter-
attack to the desire to go on existing. It will be very natural,
then, for that ego to seek the quest or to seek the spiritual
path to find its way out.

There is a story in *Talks with Ramana*. Somebody had re-
ported to Ramana this strange story about an Englishman
who, in England, happened to look at a picture of Ramana
and broke out into tears. And he had no mystical inclinations
or spiritual desires one way or another. They asked Ramana
what it was about. Ramana said this man had reached that
point in his evolution and he just turned around. From then
on he just went the other way.

So it's what the Hindus refer to as the soul's inclination
towards manifestation. When it reaches a certain point, then
the inclination is to withdraw from manifestation. That means
it has to seek a path to get out.

LR: Is that the "revulsion" you refer to?

ANTHONY: Yes, that's a very fancy name they give it.
"Revulsion."

RG: Anthony, you just spoke of it as if it were the ego's
revulsion.

ANTHONY: One way to say it is that within a relatively short span of recent lives, the majority of which have been basically suffering, there will be built into the ego this residue, this counter-tendency against manifestation, the desire to find a way out. It gets deposited as a tendency within the ego and then becomes counter-productive as far as the ego is concerned.

There comes a point when the ego's development does reach what they call the turning about, turning around and desiring to find a way out.

RG: Is this also the point where egoism can stop?

ANTHONY: No. It goes on and on and on.

BS: Does cyclic existence only refer to the ego?

ANTHONY: Cyclic existence, I think, means to continue reincarnation into the ego or as the ego and in bondage to the ego.

LRW: When the ego has suffered enough and makes that turnaround, is it really the soul that makes the turnaround but the ego appropriates it as its own?

ANTHONY: You think the soul turns around?

RG: Well you did speak about it as the soul's leaning towards manifestation and then away from manifestation.

ANTHONY: Yes, but when I referred to the soul's manifestation, I didn't say that the soul was differentiated and had an intellectual interest in these matters. The soul's consciousness is undifferentiated, always the same. The weight of the turning around falls on the tendencies that are inherent in the ego.

Again, you have to go back to the original position that we took. We spoke about the ego as a matrix of possibilities and thoughts, tendencies, right? Deposited in this matrix through the various lives that you lived are certain tendencies. And if a person spent a few lifetimes generating or profoundly experiencing these tendencies through introversion or meditation— if he persistently practices, then these tendencies will be left behind as part of the matrix of possibilities that constitutes his ego. And it is this which will, after a certain length of time, start gathering momentum and see its way out. It's still all in the ego. It's the ego that's going to go out and seek enlightenment. It's the ego that's going to enjoy nirvanic bliss—only if it gets destroyed.

FRD: With all that we've said about the ego, it's hard to believe . . .

ANTHONY: . . that it would have good tendencies?

FRD: Well, that it could want to annihilate itself.

ANTHONY: No. He says that with part of it, it wants the truth. If a person is in extreme pain, a part of him wants to annihilate that. If a person is seeking truth and recognizes that the ego is going to have to be subdued, that's feasible.

Remember, PB is giving you a general picture of the ego. It's not completely negative. There's some good to it. He even speaks about the ego as achieving impeccable manners and being ultimately refined.

EVEN irreproachable conduct and impeccable manners belong to the ego and not to the enlightenment.

(v6, 8:1.109 AND *Perspectives*, P. 105)

ANTHONY: It's the ego that does that.

AH: How can the ego decide to destroy itself? Obviously we get interested in the quest and make a commitment and then by and by we understand that that was silly; it was really the ego that made the commitment. It's like a dog chasing its own tail, or sending a thief to catch a thief.

ANTHONY: But that's the way it is, as paradoxical as it sounds. The ego is a cluster of tendencies, cravings, and so on. And there comes a point when the ego has a sufficient cluster of tendencies which want to find out about itself. So think of this as on a sliding scale. If you think of attention or consciousness as having within it a capability of assimilating the lowest dregs to the highest, if you think of consciousness containing all these different tendencies, then one can see easily enough that the ego could reach a certain maturity where the tendencies to seek out truth or to seek goodness can become predominant. I don't see why you say "take a thief to catch a thief." That's all nonsense—who else is going to do the work?

It's better to keep to the paradoxical nature of the problems we're confronted with in trying to understand the ego than to throw it out or to make out they don't exist. This *is* my ego. This is the way it is. It's a bundle of contradictions. On one hand it desires the good but on the other it doesn't hesitate to steal or to rob or to do whatever it thinks would give it happiness. Is this so?

AH: Yes.

ANTHONY: Is it possible for me to affirm, more and more, the tendencies towards the good rather than the bad? Well, then this will make sense of education, culture, civilization. That's what it's all about, to strengthen these tendencies and weaken the others. But if this process continues—and it can continue indefinitely and for a very long time—then it's the ego that has to struggle with itself.

On the other hand, you have no guarantee of what's around the corner, let alone the next life. [*pause*] Or tomorrow. As crystallized as your ego is, it could be pretty thoroughly crushed within a few minutes.

> WHEN A MAN can forgive God all the anguish of his
> past calamities and when he can forgive other men and
> women for the wrongs they have done him, he will
> come to inward peace. For this is what his ego
> cannot do.   (v6, 8:4.349)

ANTHONY: Am I going to be angry with God until I forgive Him?

NG: It seems likely.

ANTHONY: And he says I can't forgive Him because the ego by definition won't forgive Him. When he can forgive Him, he's not there. What does that mean?

FRD: The ego's not the one that does the forgiving, obviously.

ANTHONY: Ah, you're catching on. The ego doesn't forgive anyone. How often have you spontaneously forgiven someone who has hurt you deeply? Can you count the times? Well, that's how often you were enlightened.

DB: It doesn't seem like the ego's capable of doing anything except holding a grudge.

ANTHONY: You're catching on. Get your ego out of the way, then something in you can forgive.

Maybe you have noticed that if you forgave somebody, it wasn't *you*? Now, we're talking about when you got hurt, we're not talking about somebody hitting you with a fly swatter. We're talking about you really getting hurt and you forgive them. Is it you? Have you noticed *who* it was? Let's go on to something else. You see the way the ego takes over, it takes credit: "I forgive you."

BS: Perhaps we can't understand what the act of true forgiving means. I know you say, well that's when you weren't yourself. You weren't the ego at that time. You were inspired from the Overself.

ANTHONY: That was like being nothing in front of the other person. I'm sure we all at one time or another, must have had it, must have felt it. Usually it's accompanied by the feeling, "Oh, ain't I great!" That's of course something else. But if the forgiveness is really there, and spontaneous, you will see it's the higher part of you. It's certainly not your ego.

In that moment you had forgiveness. Or forgiveness was given. But how could the ego, by definition, be selfless? How could it forgive?

BS: I'm probably trying too hard to see the point.

ANTHONY: There's some subtlety here. The statement you made was adequate and comprehensive. The moment of self-lessness is when the act of forgiveness can take place. You may regret it when the ego comes back.

MB: I know many people who have been through difficult times and have become agnostic. They feel that if there were a God, He certainly wouldn't have allowed these things to happen—things like wars that are hard to reconcile with the notion of a God that's good. But by becoming agnostic and clinging to anger and blame, they deny the existence of God and the possibility of any realization of God or any denial of their ego.

ANTHONY: So the ego has become very effective in maintaining that separation, hasn't it?

THE MORE he tries to fight the ego, the more he thinks about it and concentrates on it. This keeps him still its prisoner. Better is it to turn his back on it and think about, concentrate on the higher self.

(v6, 8:4.161)

AH: I don't understand that.

ANTHONY: That's very easy. When we come here and discuss the soul, you can't be looking at television. Instead of thinking about the lower ego, think about the higher self.

AH: Then the ego will say, "What a good boy am I. I'm thinking about the higher self."

ANTHONY: Not if you listen to Thomas Taylor, who keeps telling you you're the dregs of the universe.

HS: Then the ego will say, "Look how terrible I am. I'm the dregs." [*laughter*] How will you turn your back on it?

ANTHONY: Very easy. I keep telling you, you don't believe me! You get angry. You turn around and you walk away from it. That's how you turn your back on it! What do you want, a map, a diagram? Legends? It's that simple and straight-forward. When you get angry, you turn away, and you walk away, and you leave the anger where it was.

AH: Anthony, in the first part of that quote he talks about the trap of trying to discipline the ego.

ANTHONY: He's talking there about the Long Path and there he's giving you a very precise formulation of how to cut the whole problem by turning your back on these things. If you keep trying to think of how you can straighten out your ego, you'll be forever involved. If you just turn your back on it and do the things that really matter, you won't have to worry about straightening out the ego—except a little bit. [*laughter*]

> So LONG as we maintain our foolish self-sufficiency,
> our independence of the divine source, we must
> expect to be left to manage living with these
> limited resources.
>
> (UNPUBLISHED)

> A MAN begins to come into his own the day he rejects
> the ego. His rejection may not last more than a minute
> or two, for the false self is strong enough to reclaim its
> victim. But the process has started which will bring
> it to an end.   (v6, 8:4.162)

DB: Was that quote saying something to the effect that we're doing all this to ourselves, all the time? We actually make the decisions?

ANTHONY: Why do you think you're always angry at God?

AH: Is it that we do it to ourselves? Is it that we do it with every thought?

ANTHONY: With every breath!

AH: Every single thought keeps doing it.

ANTHONY: Remember when Plotinus asked, "What makes our souls leave the *Nous*?" [the intelligible world]. He says it's self-audacity.

AH: Are there any thoughts that don't do that?

ANTHONY: If it's a thought, it's doing that.

IF WE COULD pin down this sense of "I"-ness which is behind all we think, say, and do, and if we could part it from the thoughts, feelings, and physical body by doing so, we would find it to be rooted in and linked with the higher Power behind the whole world.

(v6, 8:1.134 AND *Perspectives*, P. 102)

ANTHONY: Isn't he saying there in a nice easy way that you know why the world is the way it is and why you're angry at it? Doesn't it come to that? There's something in the ego that recognizes the Higher Power in a very perverse way. And this recognition is why the ego could never forgive the God or the Father or whatever the Power is that made that world, because It certainly didn't make the world according to the ego's desire.

JFL: The ego has its source in the Overself and is fed by the infinite?

ANTHONY: By the same power that made the world. It's part of the cosmic circuit. It's part of the World-Idea.

JFL: As you take the file and file down the metal . . .[1]

ANTHONY: . . . as you thin down the ego . . .

JFL: . . . you're in an area where it has a hang line, a narrow support. You're going to jump off this little thing it's hanging on to?

ANTHONY: It's not going to jump off. It's not going to do it voluntarily.

JFL: Let's say it gets pulled out from under him.

ANTHONY: That could bring about an intense meditation but it could also bring about a pathological conflict. For you to engage in the conflict, withdrawing from the ego-will brings about a pathological conflict. I mean it's usually brought about that way. You're not going to go in there and say, "I'm going to have fifteen rounds with you."

JFL: Where is this battle being staged?

ANTHONY: The battle will take place in you. You'll know it. It'll be brought about. There are very rare exceptions. Remember the story of when Ramana took three things—a cigar, a ring, and something—threw them on the ground, and stepped on them. That was the announcement that it was over.

Prior to that, you know, he had said he wanted to experience death, he had brought that on almost, because there was that maturity. Remember, he decided that he wanted to experience and see what death was. He lay down in the corpse posture, put himself into trance, and there—right then and there—he conquered the ego.

I think those kind of people are rare. Most of us do it the other way. It's going to happen *to* us. That's why I don't like to talk about surrender because it's really a paradoxical thing. Very paradoxical.

WHEN THE EGO is brought to its knees in the dust,
humiliated in its own eyes, however esteemed or feared,
envied or respected in other men's eyes, the way is opened
for Grace's influx. Be assured that this complete humbling
of the inner man will happen again and again until he is
purified of all pride.   (v6, 8:4.430 AND *Perspectives*, P. 98)

OUT OF this ego-crushing, pride-humbling experience
he may rise, chastened, heedful, and obeisant to the
higher will.   (v6, 8:4.431)

DB: Is there some way to bring on this experience, since it is so beneficial?

ANTHONY: You're going to go out and seek that? Who are you, Saint Francis?! We're speaking about an ego-crushing experience! You're not going to come out better for it, you're going to come out a little humble. That's called eating crow. If you didn't eat crow, then it's not the ego-crushing experience he's talking about. Once that happens there is something made available. You are opened up a little bit, but usually it takes the whole cosmos to do it.

DB: So it's not anything you could bring about, to sit down and say, well today I'm going to crush my ego.

ANTHONY: The ego's saying I'm going to crush myself, right? If you're like Saint Francis or blessed Henry Suso, who wore a hair jacket with nails sticking into his flesh for twenty years, then you can say that. But for most of us it has to really be delivered. We're put through it. It's an ego-crushing experience he's talking about. He's not talking about what you and I think we can do.

It's true that it can be conceived of as some sort of Grace; but I think what he's trying to make clear here is that only when the ego has been humbled and its arrogance is brought to toe may the possibility of Grace come in. But as long as the ego has that persistent arrogance and a whole network of defense mechanisms to block out anything from coming in, it's not going to get that Grace; so the world has to come and crush it so that a little Grace might come in. But no one willingly goes out to seek it, take my word for it.

There are some heroic souls, I wasn't exaggerating—whether Saint Francis or Henry Suso or any of those people. But they're rare. For most of us, it's got to happen *to* us.

IF HE IS willing to look for them, he will find the hidden workings of the ego in the most unsuspected corners, even in the very midst of his loftiest spiritual aspirations. The ego is unwilling to die and will even welcome this large attrition of its scope if that is its only way of escape from death. Since it is necessarily the active agent in these attempts at self-betterment, it will be in the best position to take care that they shall end as a seeming victory over itself but not an actual one. The latter can be achieved only by directly confronting it and, under Grace's inspiration, directly slaying it; this is quite different from confronting and slaying any of its widely varied expressions in weaknesses and faults. They are not at all the same. They are the branches but the ego is the root. Therefore when the aspirant gets tired of this never-ending Long Path battle with his lower nature, which can be conquered in one ex-pression only to appear in a new one, gets weary of the self-deceptions in the much pleasanter imagined accomplishments of the Short Path, he will be ready to try the last and only resource. Here at long last he gets at the ego itself by completely surrendering it, instead of preoccupying himself with its numerous disguises—which may be ugly, as envy, or attractive, as virtue.

(v6, 8:4.167 AND *Perspectives*, P. 96)

NH: That's the point! It's as if the ego is the active agent in both paths.

ANTHONY: Both the Long Path and the Short Path are in the imagination.[2] The problem is, what is the nature of self surrender?

LR: The ego is not the active agent in that surrender.

ANTHONY: You can't say that until after.

LR: But what I've understood is that it's more like the in-flux of Grace.

ANTHONY: What's the influx of Grace?

LR: That you could surrender.

ANTHONY: No, better turn around. What is the nature of this surrender? Let's get to the point. What is the nature of self-surrender? When all is said and done, this is what you've got to fundamentally do.

AH: This confrontation is beyond both paths and different than any path. This is the fundamental confrontation . . .

ANTHONY: No, what is it?

AH: It's death, from one point of view.

ANTHONY: It's worse than death, because when you die you're going to come right back. You did not give up the ego, so you're going to come back. So it's not like death. Very few people really die, believe me.

AH: Physical death is easy compared to this death.

ANTHONY: Death! Death! Very few people really die. Why? Because they haven't given up the ego. Then what do we mean when we say surrender the ego?

D: You mean totally annihilate it?

ANTHONY: It's a good thing to think over. You're not going to get it in one night.

FD: I may not ever get it.

ANTHONY: Think about it. It's very healthy.

AH: What is the "large attrition" referred to in the quote —when he says that "the ego is unwilling to die and will even welcome this large attrition of its scope if that is its only way of escape from death"? The larger field of philosophic ideals?

KD: Maybe it's associated with the "lofty aspiration" he mentions just before that. The lofty aspiration would be a thought-desire and that would be the ego.

TS: Insofar as aspiration is a thought or an emotion in the mind, and there is an impersonality to the thought or emotion, there is a certain attrition to the scope of the ego.

ANTHONY: Like in the case of a saint, the dominance of the ego is considerably reduced. In the case of an advanced mystic, it is even more reduced. But the point is that it doesn't let go. It is willing to lose some of its power rather than be annihilated. So it will give up some of its power, a little bit at a time, and in that sense it is reduced in size or it is reduced in power. You would expect from a saintly man or an advanced contemplative that there would be less egoism in him. Let's re-read some of the quote.

> . . . Since it is necessarily the active agent in these attempts at self-betterment, it will be in the best position to take care that they shall end as a seeming victory over itself but not an actual one . . .

ANTHONY: Do you follow that?

AH: Is it that the ego imagines it has conquered itself?

ANTHONY: It doesn't imagine; it *knows* it hasn't conquered itself. It's going to make *you* think it's conquered itself. Like let's say you're carrying out a certain exercise; let's say you're breathing in strength or holiness or peace. In the act of breathing in, the ego is the agent and to that extent it will modify the cosmic forces coming into you. It will *modify* them according to its own standard and its own rights, its own way of understanding these things, which will mean that it should never be annihilated. So it's the agent, the agent in the process of you trying to be better. Consequently, insofar as it's the agent, it controls the situation.

KD: That breathing in, even without images—you're saying the very act of breathing in modifies that?

ANTHONY: Yes.

KD: Even without thought?

ANTHONY: Well, without thought I don't know that you'd be using the exercise. But let's speak about a person doing an exercise—it doesn't matter what the exercise is—and in the process, as she says, "I breathe in," she imagines that she's breathing in holiness or strength or whatever quality she wishes to improve. The act of breathing in is an act by an agent, the ego. It's like a filter. What it breathes in is filtered according to its own make-up. It isn't that it's going to let those cosmic currents come in pure and clean without filtering them. So it always is in control, even in the process of trying to reach *nirvana.*

AH: So the ego makes absolutely sure the victory is a seeming one.

ANTHONY: Yes. The ego isn't going to preside over its own annihilation, of course. One would assume automatically that it's going to interfere in some way or another to prevent that from happening. Can you imagine the ego saying, "Here I am; now I'm going to get rid of myself"?

AH: That's the paradox.

ANTHONY: No, that's not a paradox; that's a *lie.* It's not going to do it, ever. It's *never* going to do that.

BS: The ego can't do all these things. The ego cannot be the one to annihilate itself. Once you even speak about annihilating the ego, it's an affirmation of the ego.

ANTHONY: Yes. Not only that, it's not going to submit to that.

BS: It seems you cannot directly attack the ego.

ANTHONY: It isn't a question of directly attacking the ego. The way to put it is to say that the ego will not destroy itself. Even if you're in the process of going through certain spiritual disciplines which are attempting to reduce the ego's strength, the ego will resist. It will be very subtle about its resistance. It doesn't necessarily have to express it or show it. But it will be there, and it will do everything it can to prevent that.

BS: But if spiritual disciplines are to have any validity, they should not be *able* to affirm the ego.

ANTHONY: You're separating the discipline from the person who does it, as though they are two things. They're not. It's one thing you're speaking about. The person who is carrying on the discipline is one thing, not two things—a discipline and a person.

BS: Is the person equatable with the ego?

ANTHONY: Yes. How effectual the disciplines or the means are towards spirituality depends upon the person who's using them. To that extent they're effectual or not effectual. Now, let's say the more gross the ego, the less effectual these disciplines are going to be. The more refined the ego, the more effective they're going to be. But you can't separate the discipline from the person who's doing the discipline. There is no objective discipline. It just doesn't mean anything.

The mystic consciously disciplines himself, and he's aware also of the interferences that are constantly emanating from his ego. If he's any kind of a mystic, he's aware of that. He'll notice the intrusions and the subterfuges and also the camouflaging that's going on all the time—the way the reason will be distorted to accommodate the ego. These are things that one notices.

> ... The latter [an actual victory] can be achieved only by directly confronting it and, under Grace's inspiration, directly slaying it ...

ANTHONY: Here's the point where you reach a certain level or a certain stage of contemplative exercise and it's taken out of your hands. It's the King within that starts guiding the whole process, the individual ego would never be able to do it. That Grace takes over and directs, and of course you'll be aware of that intuitively, that it's doing it.

[*Remainder of the quote is re-read*]

HS: Would a saintly man and a man not so versed in the

virtues both be confronting, both be approaching that same "I-thought"?

ANTHONY: I think what you're asking is: What is this ego that is going to be slain? What is it?

HS: I wouldn't know how to answer.

ANTHONY: It would be very hard to slay it, then, wouldn't it, if you don't know what it is?

Perhaps under certain situations where the total personality operates, or the total man is operative, under circumstances of that nature, sometimes, I think we become aware of what we might call our innermost "I." I think most of us have a feeling for that. It's buried very deeply within us, and you have to really use a lot of excavation to get to that "I" that I really am. Most of us are aware that we have such a thing. Can you give it up? It's not very clear while we're living the psychological life.

Imagine that we could leave that behind and go to a life that is more spiritual in the sense that we're living in the subtlety of the mind. And imagine that it's possible to go beyond that to a point where we would say that the entire processes of knowledge which have taken place are for the reason of that consciousness fulfilling itself through those thoughts. As we're tracing back this I-thought, it becomes ever more and more ethereal and refined and difficult to pinpoint because it's no longer a thing; it becomes really a state. Within the psychological state, that I-ness is relatively undefined, not very articulate. But as we advance into more mystical states, that becomes more and more defined and more and more felt, so we become identified with an infinite existence.

The next step is to give that up. And you won't. No one will give that up. A situation has to be brought about where you're forced to choose between identifying with that I-ness or dropping it. The analyses from the psychological level just are inadequate.

I don't think I could go further. But there is something in us which takes charge and *knows* and can distinguish between the profoundest subtleties of the ego and the non-ego. One has to deliver oneself completely to that guidance. I can't say more than that.

> EVERYTHING that intrudes upon the mental stillness in this highly critical stage must be rejected, no matter how virtuous or how "spiritual" a face it puts on. Only by the lapse of all thought, by the loss of all thinking capacity can he maintain this rigid stillness as it should be maintained. It is here alone that the last great battle will be fought and that the first great fulfilment will be achieved. That battle will be the one which will give the final deathblow to the ego; that fulfilment will be the union with his Overself after the ego's death. Both the battle and the fulfilment must take place within the stillness; they must not be a merely intellectual matter of thought alone nor a merely emotional matter of feeling alone. Here in the stillness both thought and emotion must die and the ego will then lose their powerful support. Therefore here alone is it possible to tackle the ego with any possibility of victory.
>
> (v15, 23:8.153 AND *Perspectives*, P. 328)

FDS: Is the stillness itself a state still within the ego?

ANTHONY: You'll never experience your ego as stillness, never in a million years. The ego by definition is nothing but a washing machine. [*laughter*]

FDS: Isn't it true that you could be in a still state of mind and not really be in the presence of the Overself?

ANTHONY: You wouldn't be in the ego if you were in a still state of mind.

RG: The fact that there's a battle doesn't mean that the ego is the stillness, it means the ego would be a content or a thought to that stillness in the battle.

ANTHONY: We're speaking about *nirvikalpa*, we're speaking about the stillness. And if you're stationed there for a while, let's say more than a couple of minutes, where is your ego going to hide?

FDS: There's no place.

ANTHONY: It seems that the framework and context in which surrender takes place are being discussed, but we're still not saying what surrender is. What are you asked to do when he speaks about surrender?

You're in the stillness, you're absolutely quiet. You're meditating. You're there for a little while. It can't hide very long there because that's like space. If there's anything, it's going to show, you're going to see it. What must inevitably happen?

RG: Thought must appear.

ANTHONY: If you're in the stillness, sooner or later thoughts are going to appear. What do you do?

FDS: You don't have to follow them up, you don't have to identify with them or anything. You can just go on.

RG: You have to push them out again. It's a great battle, he says.

ANTHONY: What kind of thoughts do you think would be in that realm? Do you think it's going to be thoughts about paying next month's rent?

RG: The root ego thought would appear.

ANTHONY: So the root ego thought appears. Could you say more? I'm asking you *what is that*, the root thought, the root ego?

FDS: That I-thought which is part of the World-Idea.

ANTHONY: We keep going around and around.

FDS: As a separate being.

ANTHONY: You're in the stillness. The root ego appears

and it seems like some other being, good. Fine, so far. What's it look like? [*laughter*]

The middle entity is taken away. Reason and emotion are no longer of any help. If the reasoning faculty in man is what creates, perpetuates, and supplies the means for the manifestation of the ego, when that's no longer functioning the ego can't call on it for support and help. Then it only has its own self-will. The problem isn't faced in the quote.

CDA: What has its own self-will, ego or the rational soul?

ANTHONY: The rational soul makes it possible for the ego to be. And that possibility for it to be is now its own self-will. You can take away reasoning, you can take away emotion and no longer does it have these as supports, but it still will have its own self-will. This is where the surrender comes. It's not going to come by the reason or emotion. It's the self-will inherent in the ego itself that must bring itself to that situation where something is forced. If you'll read that again, I think you'll see that the quote is not facing the problem of what the surrender is.

BS: The self-will is the only remaining item of the ego? Is that the will that will surrender?

ANTHONY: What distinguishes the ego is its self-will. If you introspect into yourself, moment by moment you are actualizing yourself through that self-will, and that's what will have to surrender itself. Now, how could the self-will surrender itself? It has to be brought to do so. It can't do it on its own.

RG: Who brings it to surrender?

ANTHONY: It's usually part of the situation, the World-Idea or particular circumstances. His own higher self forces him into it. No one would go out willingly and seek that.

HIS OWN self-centeredness keeps out the light. If he himself cannot open up a free way to let it in, then grace

alone can crush his ego and thus reveal his sin and bring
about surrender. (v6, 8:4.429)

ANTHONY: Of course, anyone who gets crushed is not going to consider it as grace. I remember an interesting story of
a man who was a student of Krishnamurti for many, many
years. He had to go in for an operation and just before he
went in for the operation, the very last minute, he gave up his
ego. He had the liberating experience. It was brought on. He
didn't bring it on. It was brought on. He wasn't meditating in
a nice quiet corner. He was on an operating table. He had a
few minutes of quiet, waiting, and the struggle took place.

THE EGO in him which thinks the "I" must be rooted
out. It will be followed by the Overself, which neither
thinks discursively nor identifies itself with the outer
person whom the world considers him to be.

(v6, 8:4.451)

ANTHONY: If the Overself wasn't identified with the ego
then what would it be identified with, if anything? It's capable
of absolute impersonality.

RC: You mean what content would it have?

ANTHONY: Yes, I don't know if the word is "identified,"
but what would it be associated with? If it doesn't identify
itself with the outer person then what would its point of
view be?

VM: It would be universal.

ANTHONY: It would be the World-Idea, sure. That's why
it's capable of absolute impersonality. Your Overself is not
identified with your ego because that would be discursive-
ness. What is its functioning? That's why the sage is absolutely
impersonal. He's not identified except with the World-Idea.

RC: Which would include the ego?

ANTHONY: Yes. Don't go to the other extreme and make the ego a nonentity.

DB: How does "the ego which thinks the I" differ from the I-thought?

ANTHONY: The I-thought is that light which is present in the structure of the ego. The ego thinking itself to be the I is an entirely different set-up. They're two different things.

DB: It seems that the grace which makes possible the surrender of that ego's self-will is going to permit that light to no longer be entangled within it.

ANTHONY: But the emphasis has to be put on the self-will cancelling itself out, not on the light which illuminates its activity.

DB: Can it be said that in the final analysis the fact that the ego tries to eliminate itself or tries to eliminate the self-will is due to the presence of that light?

ANTHONY: I don't buy final analysis. You're bringing up the notion of the surrender of the ego and I'm putting it in the context where it belongs—that is, in the activity of the ego itself. Its own self-will is what has to be surrendered or cancelled out. The light that happens to permeate it is not involved in the surrender. It has nothing to do with the surrender, although the surrender will take place within that light.

DB: Is it to that light that the surrender is taking place?

ANTHONY: No, here it becomes meaningless.

HS: Earlier you said that thought and emotion seem to be other than the ego, other than the I-thought itself.

ANTHONY: I pointed out that the reasoning soul is what fabricates the ego and ultimately it invests the ego with its capacity to think. And if you enter or are on the verge of *nirvikalpa* or on the threshold of stillness, you've gone beyond the reasoning phase of the soul. And that means that the reasoning phase of the soul is looked upon for what it is. You see soul has that phase which reasons. This is no longer going to be capable of offering support to the ego's self-perpetuation because you have made the distinction between what the ego is and that which brings it into being as a sensible thing. So then the ego won't be able to call on support from the reason or feeling.

HS: Then the reasoning phase of the soul is actually prior to the ego thought.

ANTHONY: That goes without saying, doesn't it? It brings about what you call your empirical ego. You think yourself into actuality, into sensible corporeality.

HS: How does the ego thought get differentiated from the reasoning phase of the soul which is thinking it into corporeality? Are you saying that there's a retraction of the subjectivity?

ANTHONY: No, there's no retraction. There's a clear distinction between the ego and the impersonal reasoning processes, or, if you want to use another term, transcendental or *a priori* synthetic reasoning that brings that ego about. You have to think hardness into existence in order to have the experience of hardness. You have to think the ego into existence in order to have the experience of ego.

HS: OK, then it's possible to have its source cut off from it or differentiated from it.

ANTHONY: One distinguishes them. Then you have isolated the ego from the reasoning processes and now you've traced it back to its lair.

HS: You traced it back to its lair but it still has its innate capacity to perpetuate itself. When it's traced back that way and isolated, is that where you get introduced to terms of surrender?

ANTHONY: No, that introduces you to what it really is. You're still not in the battle. You're still not in conflict with it. Still no conflict going on.

HS: You're differentiating the ego from the reasoning

phase of the soul and you're saying that is still prior to the battle.

ANTHONY: Yes, this can go on without you surrendering anything. It's part of the mystical understanding.

HS: Now, if you want to take up the battle . . .

ANTHONY: You don't take it up. It happens.

HS: If it happens, now the ego has been reappropriated or has been given back to its source?

ANTHONY: No. Now, it stands alone and isolated. Separated off from everything else. The point I'm making is: Now that you're encapsulated within that, what do you do? Are you willing to give it up? No. Of course not, because the only thing that surrounds you is nothingness and an abyss. You're encapsulated now in the ego structure which we distinguished and separated off from the reasoning phase of the soul and the higher phase of the soul and you're going to surrender?! You won't do it. You might be forced into doing it and then your prior discipline and training might come to your aid, but you're not going to do it willingly.

The important thing is to see that you stand alone in that isolated capsule and that within, there, is where the self-will is going to try to surrender itself. But what will it surrender to? How will it cancel itself out? To whom? PB says to the higher self. Right. But when you're in there you don't know that there's a higher self. You're going on, like blind flying. Instrument flying. Think about it.

NG: May I ask a question about what you said earlier? Does the I-thought have that light inherent in it?

ANTHONY: It depends on the context in which a thing is said. More often than not, when PB speaks about the I-thought, that's the light that's shining in the ego which makes the ego think that it is this I. The ego appropriates that light and now conceives of itself as itself. But that I-thought, that light, is not the same as the ability of the ego to perpetuate itself by discursively thinking itself into being. They're two different things.

NG: So when PB in the quote ["If he is willing . . ."] speaks about that final confrontation with the root . . .

ANTHONY: It's what we were just speaking about—this ability of the ego to perpetuate itself by discursively thinking itself into being, constantly. Now, we're only abstractly separating the light from that. You can't do it in actuality because there wouldn't be any consciousness in the ego that would make it aware of its own activities. It's a very messy affair.

AP: Could you explain more what you mean by reason?

ANTHONY: There are different phases of the soul that we speak about in the Plotinus class—different phases of the soul that a person who is a proficient becomes aware of. There is a reasoning phase of the soul which we can call a sort of permanent witness; there's the supreme subject, the Overself; and then there's the empirical ego. Plotinus speaks about these in various ways. Now the fact that he made these distinctions about one and the same entity means that he was able to stand apart and see them as different from one another.

AP: Does the reasoning phase back up the ego?

ANTHONY: That's always backing you up. You're always calling on it to make sure that you have your way. I think it was Freud who claimed that reasoning is nothing but self-rationalization. He was partly right.

JC: Anthony, you're saying that the ego appropriates that reason in the same way that it appropriates the light.

ANTHONY: Exactly, the way it appropriates the light.

BY THOUGHT, the ego was made; by thought, the ego's power can be unmade. But the thought must be directed toward a higher entity, for the ego's willingness to attack itself is only a pretense. Direct it constantly to the Overself, be mentally devoted to the Overself, and emotionally love the Overself.

Can it then refuse to help you?   (v12, 18:1.77)

HS: You said if a person takes one step toward the Overself, it takes ten steps toward the person.

ANTHONY: Yes, but you have to take that one step. Remember the quote I like best: "The ego worships itself."

This whittling away of the ego may occupy the entire lifetime and not seem very successful even then, yet it is of the highest value as a preparatory process for the full renunciation of the ego when—by Grace—it suddenly rises up in the heart.   (v6, 8:4.422)

CDA: What rises up in the heart?

ANTHONY: When the time comes, it'll arise. Learn to see what he's saying. "One more time," sure. Just one more time. Here I am, sixty, still with the same habits, "Just one more time, one more year," and they're still there, then eighty, "Just one more time," and they're still there. [*laughter*] Isn't he saying simply, "Keep at it. Don't stop."

AS: I thought he was talking about Catch-22: You *have* to do all this work to try and try and whittle away the ego, but *that* work will never actually finish the job. And if you don't do all that work, then that which *can* finish the job won't become activated, won't arise.

ANTHONY: When the time comes, if you haven't done that work you won't know it. But if you have done that work, and there comes the moment where the situation arises where you have to surrender the ego, that makes it possible for you to give up the ego—or at least recognize that this is what's being called for. But you have to do the work first.

You're not going to give up the ego just like that—I mean, as if all of a sudden you're presented with a situation where you can give up the ego and the Void Mind knows itself. These things don't happen like that.

Here I am, sixty-two, and I've still got the same habits. I can't get rid of them. But that should be no excuse for me to stop. Because I know what I'm dealing with. And this ego will never say, "Well, all right, I'll let you win this round." Never. So I just have to keep trying. But an occasion may arise, when the possibility of surrendering the ego will take place: in meditation, some crisis, or something. And if you haven't struggled all the time with it, you certainly will not at that time attempt to surrender it.

LG: What is the renunciation that rises up in the heart?

ANTHONY: That's the only place it can come. It can't come in your head. If you're thinking about it it's not there.

AH: How could the ego wish for its own annihilation? Only grace could provide that.

ANTHONY: PB remarks that there are egos so rich in experience that they reach the point of satiation and just naturally surrender. We spoke before, for example, of Ramana Maharshi. At a young age he thought, "So, what's this all about?" He lay down thinking, "Let me see what it is to die."

But don't you try it. It won't work. You know, that's an old, ripe soul. Sixteen years old, he's had enough.

PA: Is it possible this surrender can take place in a graded, gradual way?

ANTHONY: Surrender doesn't have to be when you're meditating, by the way.

RC: It might just be in class trying to listen to something . . .

ANTHONY: That would be one of the graded surrenders. [laughter]

THE subjugation of his ego is a Grace to be bestowed on him, not an act which can be done by him. (v6, 8:4.413)

ANTHONY: Subjugation of the ego means surrender the ego. Go on. Just in case you think *you're* going to surrender the ego!

LR: Suppose you change your focus of identity from the ego to the Overself.

ANTHONY: No, you're not going to get out of it that easy.

LR: So if you're really identified with the ego you never really surrender it. You'd have to change the ego.

ANTHONY: But you're going to try. You have to try.

LR: Is it possible that true surrender takes place without your really knowing it?

ANTHONY: Don't worry, you'll know it. It will be the most agonizing thing you've ever gone through.

REMOVE THE concept of the ego from a man and you remove the solid ground from beneath his feet. A yawning abyss seems to open up under him. It gives the greatest fright of his life, accompanied by feelings of utter isolation and dreadful insecurity. He will then clamour urgently for the return of his beloved ego and return to safety once more—unless his determination to attain truth is so strong and so exigent that he can endure the ordeal, survive the test, and hold on until the Overself's light irradiates the abyss.

(v6, 8:4.465 AND *Perspectives,* P. 99)

HE: By concept of the ego, does he mean the ego's taking itself to be a real, independent entity?

ANTHONY: Let's try examples, Harriet, of what the concept of ego is. Suppose you're walking down the street and you're young and beautiful and I see you and I whistle and you turn around and I say, "Let's go for a cup of coffee," and you say, "Sure." We go for a cup of coffee. I feel a certain arousal. Or let's say I'm window shopping and I look at this mohair black suit and I imagine myself dressed in it. "Oh, boy!" Or I'm walking down the street and there's this huge luxurious car and I see myself driving down Route 96 with everyone looking at me—especially the questers! [*laughter*]

I think this is the concept of the ego. It's hard to get to it by words, but I think we are all familiar with the feeling. I take you for coffee and I have this feeling that I am, I'm something, I'm someone. Can you imagine living without that? It's pretty hard. Most of us would think it's just impossible.

We're saying that in each and every one of us there is this craving, this desire, for existence. And it manifests through whatever that thing that we're craving for is. So it could be that beautiful car, that girl, that object of desire. Through each and every one of those objects of desire, my craving for existence gets manifest. It's that very craving which I think he's referring to as the ego, the concept of the ego. And if you get to that, if you could pull that out, it's a crucifixion. It's really quite a job. So I think that way we get closer to what this concept of the ego is. Because every time we have an encounter with it, we lose. As soon as you try to argue with it, it's over.

DB: Assuming that one has this experience—where this craving has been torn out temporarily or stopped—the normal response to that experience is going to be absolute, abject terror.

ANTHONY: No. It's usually detachment, renunciation. If you go through any experience of grief—for instance, if you lose a beloved—all of a sudden the world gets absolutely deglamorized and you no longer care. I'm not saying it's going to last. Tomorrow it will resume. You know that feeling where any kind of existence that would be offered just has lost all value.

DB: I had an experience like this where everything was devalued and I thought I was going to the other place. It was very frightening.

ANTHONY: You thought you were going bananas?

DB: Yes. How do you deal with that?

ANTHONY: You don't deal with it, you go through it. Let's try to explain it, because these things are difficult. All of us at some time or another have gone through something like that.

Let's say a person goes through a heart attack, where he experiences momentarily a complete withdrawal. Then he comes back and resumes life but something has happened. He has learned that he can be separated from everything completely within the matter of a moment and that remains behind as some kind of understanding. I'm not saying the understanding is as full as when he's going through the experience, but the experience will leave behind traces. These traces are incorporated into our understanding and gradually we begin to realize that these things can happen. And so the craving to experience the desires that we projected gets diminished gradually, little by little.

The person cannot renounce the world until sufficient experience of the transitory nature of his desires is experienced and that is dropped in his understanding, that becomes his understanding. Then he can take a renunciation. Then he can say, "I'll renounce. I'll detach." But you just can't get up and say, "Well, I'll be detached." It doesn't work like that.

So you go through these experiences. In some matters you are forced, you have no choice, you will be put through it. And you come out and, depending on whether you understand or glimpse the meaning of the experience or not, depending upon that, you will either benefit or not. When a person goes through something like that and tries to understand what was being experienced, he will benefit. The other, who resists that experience and fights back, he won't benefit. So it depends on the individual. But that's an understanding which remains permanent. It remains part of your make-up.

Now at the same time that I said this, I was saying what I was trying to tell Harriet. That is, little by little, the craving for existence which is always being manifested, constantly, by the ego, is getting reduced—little by little. It's a very difficult thing. No one willingly parts with the ego. We've been with it so long that we think we *are* that.

> THE FIRST CONTACT of the student with the Void will probably frighten him. The sense of being alone—a disembodied spirit—in an immense abyss of limitless space gives a kind of shock to him unless he comes well prepared by metaphysical understanding and well fortified by a resolve to reach the supreme reality. His terror is, however, unjustified. In the act of projecting the personal ego the Overself has necessarily to veil itself from the ego at the same time. Thus ignorance is born.
>
> (v15, 23:8.35)

ANTHONY: It's the same thing as in the dream. You project a dream and you have to distinguish the self, otherwise you won't have a dream.

LR: Wasn't there a comment that it's only after you come out that you have the fear?

ANTHONY: No, you can have the fear before, too.

LR: But what about in the experience?

ANTHONY: No, in the experience there's none.

LR: There's nothing there to experience . . .

ANTHONY: But when you approach that threshold it's like you're flying blind for a while. You set your instruments, you know the way you're going, and you just keep going. It's a strange thing, when you get in the void or you're close, there's no place for any thoughts to hide. There are no little nooks or crannies or corners, no curtains, there's no place for it to hide.

> THOSE WHO succeed in reaching this point in their meditation often withdraw just there, overcome by

terror or gripped by panic. For the prospect of utter annihilation seems to yawn, like an abyss, beneath their feet. It is indeed the crucial point. The ego, which has lurked behind all their spiritual aspirations and hidden in disguise within all their spiritual thinking, must now emerge and show itself as it really is. For where, in this utter void, can it now conceal itself?

(v15, 23:8.38)

ANTHONY: That *is* an experience. When you're at the Void, there's no place you can hide any more. How could the ego get into the nothingness?

AH: Is that the stage where it would be possible for the ego to manifest as "the dweller?"

ANTHONY: Oh, no, you've gone past "the dweller."

But this is the stage where the ultimate nature of the ego comes out. Here you see the *roots* of fear. Here and here only will you see where fear really is—where it has sprung from. And it is probably the most basic emotion in the ego complex's history.

The utter annihilation that he speaks about here is not like the annihilation that you experience when you're going to die. Because when you're going to die, there's almost a hidden certainty that you won't die—something like the ego knows it won't die, it'll just reappear, come back again in a different way. But the utter annihilation he speaks about here is that the very root-nature of the ego faces its own extinction. It's a different kind than when a person dies. A person dies with hope; there, there's no hope.

Most of us hear about annihilation—a person dies—but I think buried deep in our heart everyone is aware of the fact that one way or another he'll turn up, whether it's as a carrot or an apple or an orange or a turnip [*laughter*]; he'll turn up again. Here, he cannot turn up again. So the word here is very precise: *utter* annihilation. The ego is dismantled at its very root. That's why those people who have this experience and come back in a sense have no ego, as we understand it. We just don't know what that is, the way *we* understand it. I mean, they don't experience it and feel it the way we feel it.

Thought is a kind of self-will. These are things you begin to perceive after a while. Your mind is like an organ; just like your eye can see the pole, see colors. After a while your mind gets like an organ of perception. It sees these thoughts and perceives the actual functioning.

And that is always the better way, because it's easier to do something once you understand that this is what has to be done. That's why when we spoke before about the fact that you perceive the imbecilic situation that you're in, with this ego always chattering away—when you perceive that it's actually this way, then it's easier to make the effort to stop the chattering. Whereas if someone tells you, "Stop thinking," it's much harder, because you're just taking it on his say-so that it's going to lead to something. But if you see for yourself, then you will more readily and easily do it. You'll be self-convinced. This is the way.

RC: Here is a quote from Edward Conze in *Buddhism: Its Essence and Development* (pp. 22–23):

> . . . there is in the core of our being a basic anxiety, a little empty hole from which all other forms of anxiety and unease draw their strength. In its pure form, this anxiety is experienced only by people with an introspective and philosophical turn of mind, and even then only rarely. If one has never felt it oneself, no amount of explanation will convince. If one has felt it, one will never forget, however much one may try. It may come upon you when you have been asleep, withdrawn from the world; you wake up in the middle of the night and

feel a kind of astonishment at being there, which then gives way to a fear and horror at the mere fact of being there. It is then that you catch yourself by yourself, just for a moment, against the background of a kind of nothingness all around you, and with a gnawing sense of your powerlessness, your utter helplessness in the face of this astonishing fact that you are there at all. Usually, we avoid this experience as much as we possibly can, because it is so shattering and painful. People who are busy all the time, who must always think of something, who must always be doing something, are incessantly running away from this experience of the *basic* or *original* anxiety. What we usually do is to lean and to rely on something else than this empty centre of ourselves. The Buddhist contention is that we will never be at ease before we have overcome this basic anxiety, and that we can do that only by relying on nothing at all.

FRD: How would you relate the ego to the core of anxiety spoken of in this quote?

ANTHONY: Conze is talking about what the Buddhists call *dukkha.* If you are momentarily relieved of your ego, you would experience what he's talking about. It would be like an abyss opening up. The momentary removal of a person's ego is the experience of the greatest dread and fear you could know. When it comes back you embrace it, you love it, you glorify in it. The point I'm trying to get at is: What was that experience? Right then and there.

RC: The real experience, I would say, would be an experience of the unconditioned.

ANTHONY: Yes. Wouldn't you say he momentarily experienced nothingness? The withdrawal of the ego brings about the experience of nothingness, and then there is the dread to be without your ego.

RC: Who are you saying is having this dread? What would prevent it from being an experience of great joy and freedom?

ANTHONY: From the ego's point of view, an experience of nothingness is dread.

SC: When all sensation is withdrawn, everything is withdrawn except this emptiness, and this emptiness is combined with fear and dread. Are you saying that the ego somehow is still present and that's the dread or fear?

ANTHONY: The ego is withdrawn and there is a momentary experience of nothingness. The next instant when the ego returns, it experiences the dread, the anxiety, and everything else. Why hasn't it experienced it joyfully? You answer me.

RC: I would think in that case it's because the stage in that individual's evolution is such that he is identified with the ego rather than with the higher level of experience.

ANTHONY: He's not ready. And even when he's ready he's not ready.

LR: Can you describe at what point the experience is one of light or intelligence rather than terror?

ANTHONY: When there is complete detachment from the ego, when your ego is completely cut off, completely. A partial cutoff and you would still experience dread and horror.

LR: But wouldn't that experience of the other have to take place in order to be totally cut off from the ego?

ANTHONY: Yes, but in the experience of the mystical death you are going to go through a preliminary dread, because as you approach it you become aware of it, you feel it, you know it. It is only when you are completely out of the ego that you experience the joy and the light. As long as there is even the slightest ego, even if you are at the very circumference of the ego, you'll still experience the dread. You've got to be completely out of the ego to experience the joy that you are speaking of, the bliss.

THERE IS no need to yield to the fear of the void, which
comes in the deepest meditation. That is merely the
personal ego offering its resistance to the higher self.
That same fear of never being able to come back has to
be faced by all advanced mystics when they reach this
stage of meditation, but it is utterly groundless and is
really a test of faith . . .   (v15, 23:8.62)

ANTHONY: You try to convince the ego of that!

THE DEEP realization of the unreality of ego leads at
once to sudden enlightenment. But only if this realization is maintained can the enlightenment become
more than a glimpse.   (v6, 8:4.442)

HS: When you read "unreality" there, how do you understand that?
ANTHONY: You recognize its nature to be a thought. It's
not permanent reality. It's not permanently obvious. If you
have a momentary *nirvikalpa samadhi*, where you're in a
thought-free consciousness, in the moment of exiting from it
you recognize the unreality of the ego in the sense that you
see it's just a series of thoughts. If you can hold on to that, and
not be engulfed by the wake that the ego is going to confront
you with, then you remain permanently enlightened.
HS: You would come back though?
ANTHONY: But usually when you come back you're engulfed, you're taken in, the ego really embraces you, with such
loving warmth that you go right down to the pit again.
HS: You're saying there is the possibility for the entity to
remain outside of the ego's stream even though there's a re-
entry into it?
ANTHONY: Yes.

AH: What is that identity?

ANTHONY: The identity here that he's referring to is the fact that you recognize yourself to be this pure cognitive is-ness, the thought-free state of mind. That's not really identity; this is what you are.

AH: How do you hang on to a thought-free state of mind?

ANTHONY: Because you already have disciplined the ego, and so you can tell it what to do. If you haven't disciplined the ego, you will not be able to hold on to that native identity that you are.

NH: Does that mean that the sage has to maintain constant effort?

ANTHONY: No. We said that if you already went through the discipline of putting the ego in its place, making it not tyrannize over you, making it a good servant, then you are prepared to hold on to your enlightenment. So for the sage it wouldn't be an effort, it would be a constant state of affairs. But for most of us, if we get a glimpse, we're not ready for it— and the moment the glimpse ceases we're right back inside the ego, and it has its way.

MB: What about the anxiety that arises after a glimpse like that? Is that the ego also?

ANTHONY: That's the ego, yes, making sure that you never go back there again. "That was a really dark, terrible hole."

MB: He makes the promise that this deep realization leads at once to sudden enlightenment.

ANTHONY: Sudden enlightenment simply means that you are free of the ego, and you're experiencing the mind in its thought-free state, the mind in its original condition. That's what that means. Enlightenment has to be sudden, in that way, but now it's another story to maintain it, to hold on to that situation. It will depend on the prior discipline that the ego has been put through, and understanding. All these things are necessary. You could have that enlightenment, it could endure for six months, and then you lose it again. You could have it for a day, there's no way of telling.

HS: In terms of the discussion, you were saying that sudden enlightenment is a shift towards a native identity beyond the continuum, the ego continuum. And now you're saying when the native identity shifts to come back into the continuum again . . .

ANTHONY: If you're in a thought-free state, there are no thoughts; there's no need to get identified with anything because you are, or the mind is, in its original condition. No thoughts are being produced. But when you come out of the thought-free state, it is very easy to identify yourself again with the series of thoughts, one way or another. Either they foist themselves—foist themselves would be a good way of putting it—or envelop you and then that condition of being in a mentally thought-free state is gone. You're back in the identification or as identified within the ego. In other words, you're back into the personal mind.

HS: It's the personal mind that gets trained to not reappropriate improperly?

ANTHONY: Yes. The stream is always there, the World-Idea continues, all the time. It doesn't stop.

HS: But the stream itself could be trained, and not reappropriated.

ANTHONY: Yes, you get more and more immersed in it.

THE EGO moves through all the three states, but *Turiya* itself is motionless.   (v6, 8:1.26)

ANTHONY: The ego can reach right up into the *prajna* consciousness, and it does, to some extent, interpret what's going on there. It's obliterated in *nirvikalpa samadhi.* Before that it's still active.[3]

AT EVERY point of his progress the ego still functions—
except in deep, thought-free contemplation, when it is
suppressed—but it becomes by well-defined stages a
better and finer character, more and more in harmony
with the Overself. But total relinquishment of the ego
can happen only with total relinquishment of the body,
that is, at death.   (v6, 8:1.188)

ANTHONY: He's disagreeing with the Vedantists' concept
of liberation in life [*jivanmukta*]. He's saying that there is no
total liberation until you're dead. You can read the last two
chapters in the Guénon book *Man and His Becoming According to the Vedanta* on the two kinds of liberation: in the body
and out of the body. It's a discussion that's been going on
now in India for a couple of thousand years—whether or not
you could be liberated in the body. And there are pros and
cons on that. And he's saying no, as long as you have a body,
complete and total liberation is not there. This 2 ½ % or 3%
of the ego is retained.

HS: Could you speak a little on the part that says, "At every point . . . the ego still functions—except in deep, thought-
free contemplation, when it is suppressed"?

ANTHONY: In *nirvikalpa* there is no ego. You have complete impersonality, but in any other state you would have
some partiality, some person, some distorting.

HS: You say that's only in *nirvikalpa*, which, it seems to
me, is a total suppression of all thought.

ANTHONY: Yes.

HS: But it seems that he was referring to the idea that
the ego-thought can be held down a little and not absolutely
appropriate the thinking, and there could be a conscious
foothold within the thinking.

ANTHONY: Yes, there could be relative degrees of impersonality. Science is an example of that.

HS: OK, but science is like an abstraction of this.

ANTHONY: All I'm saying is that science attempts to be impersonal in its findings. Human beings cannot be completely impersonal because there's always some interference—what they call the personal equation or the ego. And not unless that's completely silenced would there be complete impersonality. Even in the case of the sage there is going to be some admixture of ego.

HS: But there would be the possibility of grades of impersonality.

ANTHONY: Yes. Hopefully.

VM: PB said in the second sentence that the ego becomes a finer and finer vehicle.

ANTHONY: He'll stress over and over again that the ego has to be fulfilled. He's not going to say, like the Easterners, "Get rid of it." He might say if you want to give it up after you develop and perfect it, then you give it up, but that will keep you busy a long time.

AB: But as long as it is utilized or employed, as long as the ego is, there's a limitation on knowledge.

ANTHONY: There's no way around it. That's why in the expressions that come to us from various sages there will always be some disagreement, because of that three percent of the personal equation still functioning. You could see that when we're working with the astrological charts. Anything coming from above must manifest itself through the natal chart, that is automatically going to distort it. That's guaranteed.

DD: It doesn't ever get fulfilled, does it?

ANTHONY: It's fulfillment enough, even if you get rid of seventy percent of your ego.

EVERYTHING we do or say, feel or think is related back to the ego. We live tethered to its post and move in a circle. The spiritual quest is really an attempt to break out of this circle. From another point of view it is a long process of uncovering what is deeply hidden by our ego, with its desires, emotions, passions, reasonings, and activities. Taking still another point of view, it is a process of dissociating ourselves from them. But it is unlikely that the ego could be induced to end its own rule willingly. Its deceptive ways and tricky habits may lead an aspirant into believing that he is reaching a high stage when he is merely travelling in a circle. The way to break out of this circle is either to seek out the ego's source or, where that is too difficult, to become closely associated and completely obedient to a true Master. The ego, being finite, cannot produce an infinite result by its own efforts. It spins out its thoughts and sends out its desires day after day. They may be likened to cobwebs which are renewed or increased and which never disappear for long from the darkened corners of a room, however often they may be brushed away. So long as the spider is allowed to live there, so long will they reappear again. Tracking down the ego to its lair is just like hunting out the spider and removing it altogether from the room. There is no more effective or faster way to attain the goal than to ferret out its very source, offer the ego to that Source, and finally by the path of affirmations and recollections unite oneself with it.   (v6, 8:4.393 AND *Perspectives*, P. 95)

ANTHONY: Let's go through this, one part at a time.

Everything we do or say, feel or think is related back to the ego . . .

FD: Right away he's bringing in the three functions of the

human being: willing, feeling, and thinking. Whatever happens in any mode is related back to this initial ego.

ANTHONY: The form of perception is the ground in which willing, feeling, and knowing are operative. If you speak about consciousness or mind incarnating into a body, from that moment on, it's going to be tethered to that body. So the body is the form of perception and the willing, knowing, and feeling is going to be what the form of perception provides *to* these cognitive modes. So it's four things.

If I talk about something I know, I am talking about what I know through my body. If I talk about something I feel, it is something I feel through my body. So the body is the medium through which the experience is going to take place. It is the form of perception. These cognitive modes operate through that form of perception. Every image that is coming into your mind is going to be something that is available to knowing, willing, and feeling. That's the form of perception.

. . . We live tethered to its post and move in a circle . . .

ANTHONY: Of course you know nature has tied you to this body. Even the Vedantists are tied to the body! Everything that you are thinking about or know about or feel or will is going to be in relation to that body.

You could go beyond it. I'm not saying you've got to stick to it, but you are stuck with it to begin with, so that the entirety of all these images is going to constitute your repertoire. That is what you're tethered to, all these past images.

. . . The spiritual quest is really an attempt to break out of this circle . . .

ANTHONY: Stop right there. "The spiritual quest is an attempt to break out of this circle . . ." The circle being what?

This identification of the consciousness with the body and its functioning.

> . . . From another point of view it is a long process of uncovering what is deeply hidden by our ego, with its desires, emotions, passions, reasonings, and activities . . .

ANTHONY: That simply means that it's going to take a long time to get underneath the nature of the thought-tendencies that constitute your personality. In other words, this group of tendencies which in their togetherness constitute your personality is what you have to burrow underneath to get to the "I" that you are.

FD: So that would be a process of analyzing.

ANTHONY: You can call it the quest. It is part of the quest.

> . . . Taking still another point of view, it is a process of dissociating ourselves from them . . .

FD: "From them," I would imagine, goes back to the emotions, passions, reasonings, and activities.

ANTHONY: Dissociate from all the images that in their totality constitute what we call your repertoire, what you think you are. To dissociate from that is part of the quest.

FD: That's what you were saying before, "To know without images is to be."[4]

ANTHONY: Yes. Most people would be concerned—insofar as they are concerned with knowing, willing, and feeling—with those images that the body is providing them. Go on. You really have to sit down and meditate with these things.

> . . . But it is unlikely that the ego could be induced to end its own rule willingly. Its deceptive ways and tricky habits may lead an aspirant into believing that he is

reaching a high stage when he is merely travelling in a
circle . . .

ANTHONY: You know there are many people who, when
we have a discussion, say, "I understand you." They also assume that they have the light too. They think that the understanding is the same as the light. They say, "I understand
you." Good, fine, that's conceptual. That's not the understanding yet that I am speaking of, which is the *light* of the
consciousness. The *Bhagavad Gita* makes that into quite a
big point.

You have to be careful that when you do understand a
spiritual truth, you keep it in its proper place—that when you
understand it conceptually, you know it is conceptual understanding you have and that you have not received the *light* itself. So I could speak about the light of the understanding and
I could speak about the understanding, but they are distinct.

FD: The ego will trick me into thinking that I really know
something.

ANTHONY: Yes.

AS: Can that light of understanding also be in those three
modes or does that have to be just the pure awareness?

ANTHONY: No, the light of understanding is not pure
awareness. It is awareness but not pure awareness. It is not the
modes themselves. When you understand what that light is, it
isn't that you are thinking something or feeling something;
it is the actual light that is behind the manifested universe.

FD: But can't the light behind those three modes manifest
through one of those modes?

ANTHONY: Yes, but once it manifests through those
modes it is no longer that light. In other words, the light behind manifestation is one thing but as soon as that light gets
manifested it's another thing.

AH: Does that suggest that if you don't understand the
first one, you go in a circle? I mean, if you don't understand

the light as understanding, the light *of* the understanding, then there is a circular path you must go through. And there is no spiritual life until that light is present?

ANTHONY: I wouldn't say there is no spiritual life. It's the beginning.

AH: If I try to understand the light as spirit, I presuppose it's not the light I want?

ANTHONY: You want to get directly to the light. Why try to *understand* it as light? Get directly to it. Go directly to it.

FD: So that would be knowing without images. You would have to be that light.

ANTHONY: Yes. It's being.

. . . The way to break out of this circle is either to seek out the ego's source or, where that is too difficult, to become closely associated and completely obedient to a true Master . . .

ANTHONY: How would you ferret out the source of the ego?

SA: Observe it in action.

ANTHONY: And if you observed your mind very carefully, all day long, what would happen? Let's say you listen to a piece of music very intensely.

SA: There is a freeing.

ANTHONY: Why? You become the music. If you watch the field of consciousness very intently, you are observation. Now the next thing that you're going to see is the resurgence of the observer and the observed. And you're going to see something very curious—you're going to see that whole, that unitary consciousness, get bifurcated. You're going to see part of it identifying with the ego, or what we would call the organism. You'll see that consciousness get fragmented, bifurcated; you'll see it identify with a portion of the whole perceptual field.

HS: When you now see it identified with a portion of the whole perceptual field, have you made an advance?

ANTHONY: You will have made an advance in the sense that you notice the way the consciousness has identified with a certain cluster of sensations. And then, of course, when you're observant you'll see that this identification with this cluster of sensations is an identification with thought, memory, etc. But what would be the source of the ego?

Let's try something very, very simple. As we said before, you're listening to music, and there's a moment when you're identified with the music, and there's only the music. There is no one listening, and there is no thing listened to. It's the same thing as when you are watching something very intently; a moment supervenes where there is nothing but pure seeing or pure observation; there is neither the observer nor the observed. If you take this example, the moment when the person is nothing but pure seeing or pure observation, what will bring about the observer and the observed?

FDS: "The slightest preference, and heaven and hell are created."

ANTHONY: Don't give me a quote. Give me *your* remark.

FDS: Any localization.

ANTHONY: Any what?!

SA: Thought.

ANTHONY: Any *thought!* So then the source of the ego is *what?*

SA: Thought.

ANTHONY: No, *mistaken thought.* What did PB say there? It's very hard to ferret out the source of thought, the source of the ego, because it requires an acute analysis of your field of consciousness or the perceptions that are going on. It requires an analysis that is so acute that you actually get immersed in the perception, and you experience—again, the word "experience" here is just being transposed analogically—

but there's the experience of pure observation. In that instant of pure observation there is only one thing that will produce an ego, and that is the *mistaken habit of thinking*. That is the source of the ego.

EM: Is there any thinking that I do that isn't mistaken?

ANTHONY: Is all your thinking preoccupied or related to a center of reference which you're going to refer to as an ego?

EM: I think so. It's hard for me to think of any that isn't.

ANTHONY: Then you've answered your question.

If we can go back to the original idea—if we want to ferret out the source of the ego, and we analyze the contents of our consciousness, or we're *looking* at what's happening to us, what's right in front of us, that is the perceptual field. And you intensely and very carefully analyze it; you're preoccupied with it. You get to a point where *you* are immersed in it, to the point where there is neither the observer nor the observed. Then we could speak about just pure observation, pure seeing. That's a kind of self-absorption. What's going to break that? You start thinking again, and the whole thing starts all over again. There's a fragmentation, there's a division in the mind between subject and object. And if you have this division in the mind of a subject and an object, you have the consequences. Can you hold on to this point before you run away?

CDA: You've described thinking before as a modification going on in the bodily organism.

ANTHONY: The consciousness that permeates the brain cells, yes.

CDA: Identification with that thinking process is very mysterious to me. It's like an instant that you can never really find, that instant of identification with the thinking.

ANTHONY: Let's speak of the self in another way. You remember we said that sensations can only exist for a mind. So the sensation of white which is on a cloud a hundred miles away is something which exists within my mind, and the sensation of having an itchy toe exists within my mind. Why does my mind identify with the itchy toe and not the white cloud?

HS: Because of the habit of previously identifying with toes. [*laughter*]

ANTHONY: From its previous history. It's been doing that all along for millenniums; it's conditioned to do that and will go on doing that. Now, we're not going to be concerned about the origin of all this; we want to know how to *end* it. And that means that we have to try to find out where the source of the ego is. And if we go through this process of analyzing the entire perceptual field and then we get immersed in it, we experience ourselves as pure observation. Then, the next instant we *see*, all of a sudden, that we have identified with a certain part of that perceptual field which brings about the conflict, or the observer and the observed. And so the whole round is started again.

How you identify is not important. The fact is, you do identify. And that too is a process of thought, of mistaken thought.

CDA: You mean the identification itself is a thought?

ANTHONY: Yes, of course. What else is it?

KD: Why do you say "mistaken" thought and not just thought? Can you maintain that observation and still think?

ANTHONY: The perceptual field will continue; it will not stop. The changes in the perceptual field go on. There's the white cloud moving; now a black one comes. The perceptual field goes on, moment after moment. So we don't have to worry about the changes in the perceptual field because we're just going to assume they're going on. If we go back to the original situation: In this state where you are pure seeing, just looking, observation, why all of a sudden do you choose to identify with a certain part of that field and say, "That's me"? And as soon as you say, "That's me," then the other is going to exist, and as soon as the other exists, *samsara* [cyclic existence] is there. What went on? What went wrong? Outside of saying "mistaken thinking, wrong thinking," what else can you say brought about the ego?

JC: What about mistaken feeling? A sympathetic response?

ANTHONY: No escape is there.

JC: By "thought" you're including . . . ?

ANTHONY: Any kind of cognition and noncognition, which could be emotional. What went wrong? You were in a nice state, beautiful . . .

MB: Is it necessary to analyze the mistake itself?

ANTHONY: PB gives you two alternatives. He says either you seek out the source of the ego or you attach yourself to a master. Now the latter is very hard to come by. They're queer birds. You don't find them any more; they're extinct. And if there is one or two, I can assure you he will make sure you do not find him! So then that leaves us the other choice, right?

We have to analyze and ferret out for ourselves the very source of our ego. That is a long, laborious work, which means that you are constantly observing, watching the field where the content of consciousness is operating on a certain content, and you keep watching it very carefully. You've got to *not* intellectually understand what I'm saying; you've got to *perceive* with your mind what I'm saying. Then you say, "There I am again. Here I am all over again. Joe Doe started up again."

Have you at times noticed yourself or a child or a person who is in a state of self-absorption? You've seen your kid daydreaming, just staring off into space, and then you say, "Eat your dinner!" And all of a sudden, at that moment, he's got to come out of it. At *that moment* he's got to create an object, the dinner, and a subject who has to eat that. [*laughter*] Haven't you had lapses of memory where you just enjoy *being* without doing or thinking? We all have these occasional lapses of memory where we just *are*. At that instant, we just are.

It only takes *one* thought and the whole of heaven and hell is produced. All the conflict, anxiety, misery that we're going to know is produced by that thought. And that's why I call it *mistaken thinking*, because the thinking can go on, the thinking can go on creating the whole of the perceptual manifold, but it doesn't have to identify with a portion of that manifold.

CDA: So what you're calling the mistake is the bifurcation.

ANTHONY: Yes.

CDA: Because, if you are continually observant of the manifold, the thoughts may be of the very same nature as they might have been if you had identified with it, but there's no subject and object.

ANTHONY: And do you know what kind of world that might be?

CDA: I imagine it would be quite bright and luminous.

ANTHONY: Well, it would be quite different from the kind that we ordinarily experience in the state of fragmented or divided consciousness. Originally, this is what we're like. We're that consciousness that's undivided. But once that division takes place, then the next step follows to further and continue in this mistaken way of thinking that you are this. Now the consequence is going to follow.

The remark that the ego is that which separates itself from the universal life is a nice general statement. But I want you to go through the laborious process of thinking this out for yourself every time and every moment that you have the opportunity. Because that's the only way it's going to happen. It can't happen by parroting someone; you have to actually watch the mind doing this.

RC: In the sense that you're speaking here of ego as egoism—restrictiveness, being in the bifurcated mode, and so on—it seems that the cluster of sensations in itself is not enough to make that identification happen.

ANTHONY: Yes.

RC: The impersonal consciousness has to actually go in there and limit itself to that.

ANTHONY: That's what I meant when I said that if you're looking at the white cloud which is a hundred miles away, and here's something itching your toe, the identification is not going to take place with the white cloud—although it can, it can. Like you read about the great masters in art: They'll sit down and they'll look at a bamboo for a month before they finally paint it, because they're trying to achieve that state, divert the attention, identify with the objective. That's why generally I'm inclined to believe that Eastern art tends to be much more objective. Look at the Zen paintings. To me they seem much more objective.

The very act of identifying with the toe rather than with the white cloud isn't an inherent necessity in the toes themselves. It's the preference, the thought, which misidentifies, which wants to identify. So that's what I mean when I say that the ego is basically going to arise because there is mistaken thought.

AH: Anthony, finding the source of the ego is spoken of as being extremely difficult. It's experienced as a disaster, a catastrophe, to actually begin to do this, is it not?

ANTHONY: Yes, but you'll be forced, sooner or later, to do it, when the despair and the misery get intense enough.

LR: The surprising thing is that we don't do it more often. If you're going from a place of utter peace, contentment, serenity, wholeness, it's surprising that you wouldn't want to spend more effort staying there. The force of habit is overwhelming.

ANTHONY: Of course, you should capitalize and put in red letters "THE FORCE OF HABIT." That's why I call it mistaken thought, mistaken thinking, because people think that they can rectify that by an intellectual recognition of it. That's not so at all. An intellectual recognition is one thing, but to bend the mind to think correctly is going to require an intense period of training and preparation and constant application.

LR: And this "force of habit," isn't that the way you describe the "dragon"?

ANTHONY: Well, you certainly could use that language, but you can also think of it as a historical conditioning that's been going on for millenniums and gets harder and harder the more we participate in it. That's why it's always easier to break a habit in the beginning than after ten or twenty years.

AH: Anthony, would you mind speaking a little more about the distinction between an intellectual grasp of this issue and the seeing of it or the perceiving of it?

ANTHONY: Let's use an exaggeration. Suppose we say something like this. The mind puts together the perceived world or whatever is manifested out there for you. You say, "Well, I understand that." So I'll say, "Fine." Now suppose it was possible for me to give you a drug where the processes of the mind are so slowed down that you can actually witness the mind put together the variety of all its mnemonic deposits and make an image. And now you watch this whole process.

In the first case, it was an intellectual understanding—"Oh, sure, I understand what you mean when you say the mind puts the World-Idea together for you." In the second case, you actually *watch* the mind get all the ingredients it needs and put them together to make the picture for you. That would be to actually perceive the truth of the statement. The other would be an intellectual understanding.

AH: In the second case, the ego itself would experience a kind of disorganization. It would see itself as being put together, rather than as having a self-standing position.

ANTHONY: Yes, but the ego won't see that, because the ego is part of the thing that's being fabricated, put together.

AH: The ego can't see that.

ANTHONY: No, it can't see that. That's why a Glimpse always brings about the understanding of the illusory nature of the ego. A Glimpse will give you the actual perception of the illusory nature of the ego. That you could actually be conscious, be consciousness, and there is no ego, no structured ego there shows you that the ego doesn't have any reality, that it's only a series of thoughts. You could actually perceive that. The ego can't perceive that. That's why that's one of the most fundamental issues of mystical experience: the recognition that the ego is illusory. That is fundamental. That is one of the reasons that the Buddhists make such an issue of that.

FD: The first way, "to seek out the ego's source," seems to be speaking really directly. Like the example of Ramana, where at sixteen or seventeen, bang! He wanted to experience what death would be like and then he lay down, he analyzed the body, and the thoughts and emotions all became still, and he experienced himself as I AM, as being.

ANTHONY: So through very intense inquiry into the nature of his mind or thoughts he was led to the very source of that—in other words, to the I AM which sustained all of that. That's one way to get to it. Isn't that also the approach PB uses in *The Quest of the Overself*? "I am not my body. I am not my feelings. I am not my thoughts. I am not my perceptions." So he is analyzing the nature of mind and all its products until it takes him right to the source of this intuitive feeling of the I AM—this sense of *being* without being anything in particular.

LR: So if you can't do that you should just find a teacher?

ANTHONY: Yes, because for some people that's extremely difficult. Many people would go to Ramana and say, "Hey, I've been sitting down asking 'Who am I?' and hammering away for years and I got nowhere." And Ramana would of course say, "Oh just sit down and do it." At other times the fellow would just look at Ramana and he would know, "Well, I'll sit down next to Ramana," and he would get it that way.

In the case of Ramana, if he put his eye on you, a divine activity would automatically start, because there is no ideative activity taking place in a sage. So when he looks at you, it's just like the divine looking at you and *darshan* [a transmission of grace] can take place. But I look at you and I have all kinds of crummy ideas of what I should do, whether to kick you or pull your hair for asking me all these stupid questions. [*laughter*]

So if you won't go the first way, you go the second. You go and find a master, and you pledge your allegiance. You are devoted to him and no one else.

The point is that *satsang*, or association with holy people, is not a physical association. It is much more inward. You would know inwardly that this is your teacher. You know; your heart tells you, "This is my teacher." You don't decide to take a trip around the world as soon as you meet him. You usually stay with him unless circumstances force you to do something else.

FD: But it seems that for really dense people, physical proximity wouldn't hurt.

ANTHONY: That's a beginning, yes. PB has a note [v10, 15:2.487] where he speaks about the students gathered around Atmananda in an oval. It was a very beautiful sight. They were all looking up at Atmananda with a feeling of devotion seeking the truth. Their devotion to their teacher will eventually accrue for them what they are looking for. As Ramana says, once you have pledged to find the truth a sage is like a tiger. He will pick you up by the neck and he doesn't let you go until that is accomplished. It might take a long time but it will get done.

FD: That spreads out through your whole life even when the sage is no longer?

ANTHONY: Oh yes. There is a very esoteric quote. [v16, 25:5.274, P. 236] I was even surprised that PB had put it in the notes. He says that there comes a time when the sage is going to incarnate and a call goes out to all the corners of the universe and his students will reincarnate then. His work is very carefully organized. He has to will himself into incarnation. He has to know all these things. But when he does so the students will at that time reincarnate. I'm not saying all at the same day, at the same hour. But it's quite a good quote. It puts a feeling in your heart.

> ... The ego, being finite, cannot produce an infinite result by its own efforts ...

ANTHONY: You or I cannot, of our own will, bring about a condition known as enlightenment. That is an infinite knowledge. Only a sage can do that because only a sage himself is infinite knowledge and can produce an infinite result. But you and I as finite psychological beings cannot.

No matter how intensely the ego thinks about the Overself, the best that it can do is come up with another thought. Whereas if you sit next to a sage, what can he do? He can stop you from thinking, slow down the mental processes, and you could experience that infinite consciousness. So the sage could bring that about, whereas my ego can't bring that about.

My ego cannot produce this infinite consciousness. The best it can do is: "I have another thought—infinite consciousness, infinite knowledge." It can go on doing that forever, but never bring about its *own* cessation, whereas the sage can do that. He can produce this infinite result, this infinite activity, this infinite knowledge. Because the experience of your Overself, or the glimpse of it, is infinite. It is an experience of infinity.

> ... It spins out its thoughts and sends out its desires day after day ...

FD: It's constantly fabricating images, tendencies, and then desires.

ANTHONY: It gets so monotonous, boring—every day the same stupid thoughts, same stupid feelings.

FD: But the thing that bothers me more is that I'm still attracted to them.

ANTHONY: Even that, too, is a tendency. That attraction to these things is a tendency that you've got to recognize. It gets very, very monotonous, yes.

FD: The tendency to like them and the arisal of them would be one side . . .

ANTHONY: Even more fundamental than that is *expectancy*. You operate always with expectancy, anticipation—always, constantly. The mind is always expecting, anticipating. It's looking to an image all the time, an activity. Its own activity. So after a while you have to recognize that that activity or that expectation is probably the chief motivation of the mind's functioning. What else? I used to reduce it to expectation. You sit down, you know, try to keep quiet, "Well, why are you moving? You want something?" "Yeah, I expect something." Isn't that what you do when you walk down the street and look around? Expecting something. That's the feeling I recognize, the mind, that expectancy, anticipation. "Gimme, gimme. What is it, where is it?" Some of the Orientals just call it expectation—that's the name they give the mind, "expectation." Everything else follows that.

> . . . It spins out its thoughts and sends out its desires day
> after day. They may be likened to cobwebs which are
> renewed or increased and which never disappear for
> long from the darkened corners of a room, however
> often they may be brushed away. . . .

ANTHONY: One of the ways you can look at this is to go to

your astrological chart and read the degree symbols. Understand the way it functions and you'll see it is always doing that. There it is, it's doing it all the time, and it keeps on doing more of it. Tomorrow it'll do it, the day after, it goes on and on and on. Then you begin to see, Ah, these are the tendencies that I have, that have been reincarnated life after life and are really very strong now; they produce their own activity.

> . . . So long as the spider is allowed to live there, so
> long will they reappear again . . .

FD: So as long as this initial thought of expectancy is allowed to continually manifest and affirm itself, so long as it is allowed to keep spinning out images and desires, it's constantly going to identify with them. You can get rid of them, image by image, but as long as that primal expectancy is allowed to stay, more images will arise.

> . . . Tracking down the ego to its lair is just like hunting out
> the spider and removing it altogether from the room . . .

AH: I can see the web as the thoughts and images, but how should we understand the spider? As an entity?

ANTHONY: Yes, but a pseudo-entity. Not a real one. It has no "inherent existence." [laughs] Like I told you, if you take all these thoughts that in their togetherness constitute your astrological chart and you see it function, you'll see it's like an entity. You'll see it, every day, the stream of consciousness. You know the notion of the stream of consciousness? Well, believe me, most of the novelists never really looked into what the stream of consciousness really is or they wouldn't think it's so great.

AH: Let's say one successfully found the spider. Is that a way of speaking about the discovery of its non-inherence?

ANTHONY: Well, that is a way of speaking or recognizing that the ego is it. That's what you've got to go after. You've got to trace it all the way. Find it. And remember the only way you can really find it is to approach the confines of *nirvikalpa*. Because then it has nowhere to go, then you'll see it for what it is.

> ... There is no more effective or faster way to attain the goal than to ferret out its very source, offer the ego to that Source, and finally by the path of affirmations and recollections unite oneself with it.

ANTHONY: That would be the Short Path. Let's say that a person meditates very intensely, gets a Glimpse. Once he gets a Glimpse, he recognizes the illusory nature of the ego but also its tyrannical sway. Then usually what a person does is offer that ego to his higher self. In other words he wants to be of service to the higher power and all he can do is pray and ask that that be given for him to do. Make sure you know what you're asking for, because this is a big thing. Once you do that, I'm not saying it's granted, but then there comes a series of lives where egoism is really crushed, or you go through a training where you get rid of it, or you come across a master who will help you get rid of it.

FD: But either way it is a painful process.

ANTHONY: Of course there are some exceptions. Some people can reach it through beauty or joy. But I think that is a minority. The crushing or putting the ego down and getting rid of its tyranny is very, very difficult.

Once you find out its nature, then you can offer the ego to the Source. Now *that's* capitalized. I would call *that* Source the Overself, the higher Soul. You offer that which you have found out to the higher Soul.[5]

Once you find that consciousness, it's to that consciousness that you can offer the ego. You first have to find that the Source within you is this consciousness, because that's what's illuminating all the thought-tendencies that constitute, or are, the ego. In themselves, these thoughts are not conscious.

Imagine the imagery in a dream. The illumination of the dream is different from the images. Now if those images turn and say, "What's illuminating me? What's lighting me up?" they'd have to turn to that light, that consciousness. That's their Source.

LR: What do you mean by offering the ego to that Source?

ANTHONY: Isn't that the Bodhisattva ideal? You're offering to try to be of service. You realize the illusory nature of the ego. Now what would you do? Are you going to go around saying the ego doesn't exist? Well, what would you do?

CDA: You offer it so that it can become a vehicle.

ANTHONY: Yes, you become dedicated to the Higher. What would that mean? What is the Bodhisattva ideal? To develop wisdom and compassion until all are enlightened. Now this "mistaken way of thinking" is going to be dedicated to what?

CDA: To the enlightenment of humanity.

ANTHONY: Yes.

EM: There would have to be a dedication in a certain sense to *all* egos, rather than just to the one that you've identified yourself with.

ANTHONY: Yes. Wouldn't you say the dedication means that you are going to *direct* this ego, dedicate it to a higher ideal, a higher service? That's what the Bodhisattva ideal is, for the service and enlightenment of humanity. So that means that now *you* have to take a direct hand in guiding this karmic continuity.

It doesn't require much perception to see that once one recognizes that the continuity of the ego is something that's assured, in the sense that it will always be going on, then you have to take a direct hand in guiding its growth and evolution —not only for its own purposes but for the purposes of all humanity. I think we could put it that way.

First ferret out the source of the ego. Once you find out what it is, then you get dedicated to the service of the Higher. You recognize that thinking is what's producing the ego and that now you have to play a hand in thinking a certain way so that you produce a certain ego: That's the dedication. This thinking is going to go on; you're going to guide it, and the guidance is going to take away from it the egoism that it operates with.

RC: So when you speak about the affirmations, it's not that the person is making the statement, "I am this, that, and the other thing," from inside the ego. It's done from a perspective outside the ego, directing that thought into the ego.

ANTHONY: Of course, "inside" and "outside" are difficult but I think you're saying that you're poised at that point where thought occurs, and you guide it properly according to the ideals which have been devised by the higher powers.

RC: It's a very different thing for us, where we are now, to say, "I am Infinite Peace," because where we're standing to make the statement is the wrong place to bring about the result. But if one is standing at that point of leverage, then a thought like "I am this peace" can be directed *into* the more limited . . .

ANTHONY: I think that it would be at that point, at what you call "leverage," where we can properly speak of: "As a man thinketh in his heart, so be it with him."[6]

AS: It would be like the guy in the dream who thinks, "I am peace." He can't really think anything effectively because his thoughts are just reflective; but if he were at the point of the dreamer's mind, he would have the power to think the dream, and he could think any qualities he wanted into that dream . . .

ANTHONY: And to establish them there as part of a continuity. Do you understand the nature of the work that's laid out?

AP: No.

ANTHONY: Neither do I. I'm quitting. [*laughter*]

MB: Would detachment from your own selfish interests be part of this path, whereas detachment from your perceptual field would be an erroneous kind of detachment?

ANTHONY: That can't happen unless you go into *nirvikalpa.*

DB: How do you know whether someone who professes himself to be on the Bodhisattva path is kidding himself or not?

ANTHONY: That's a question for each person's conscience. I can't answer a question like that. I think that point is very good. Do you know when it's legitimate, when you are not kidding yourself? I think it's an important point; I don't think I could answer it. It's something that each person has to ask in his own heart. No one could determine that.

And I would go further and say that you don't even need a ceremony. When the time comes and you feel that that's the way it is, that's the way you want it, you take that vow in your heart, and it may not even be with words. It could be carried on very secretly, and in your own heart, in the depths of the stillness. It's your business from there on.

PC: I'd like to ask about two quotes. Here's the first one.

ALTHOUGH we may grant the fact that it is the ego which is seeking truth, we must insist on the completing truth that the ego is never the finder of truth.

(v6, 8:4.440)

ANTHONY: There's no conflict. That's fine. Now the other quote.

WHAT OR WHO is seeking enlightenment? It cannot be
the higher Self, for that is itself of the nature of Light.
There then only remains the ego! This ego, the object of
so many denunciations and denigrations, is the being
that, transformed, will win truth and find Reality even
though it must surrender itself utterly in the end as the
price to be paid.   (v6, 8:4.435 AND *Perspectives*, p. 97)

ANTHONY: You don't get the truth until you pay the price,
and that means you get rid of the ego.

PC: The second quote says the ego, transformed, will win
truth.

ANTHONY: Yes. The ego transformed, disciplined, purified. It is *that* which will win truth.

PC: But the first one says that the ego will *not* find truth.

ANTHONY: No, the ego cannot find truth because obviously the way it will get the truth is when it gives itself up.
Now when it gives itself up, there's no ego that wins the truth.
You want the truth, you get rid of your ego. But at the same
time you're not going to get rid of your ego until you have
sufficiently developed it, purified it, and brought it under
the higher discipline, the higher philosophy.

RG: It's in that sense you mean "get rid" of it?

ANTHONY: Actually you don't get rid of it, you have to
transform it. Remember, he makes the point over and over
again that the ego has to be evolved, matured. It won't be capable of that sacrifice until it does reach that maturity.

PC: But if there's an enlightenment which was not present
all along, it must have occurred in the ego, although not by
the ego.

ANTHONY: But it wouldn't be the unregenerate ego any
more.

[*Quote is re-read*]

This is another one of those paradoxical statements. If you

haven't examined and tried to understand the nature of paradox, this is one of those that's too difficult. If I separate the tendencies or thoughts that constitute and are constituted of my personality from the consciousness which illuminates them, I don't have an entity, I've got an abstraction. If I conjoin them with the illuminating light that illuminates and says, "Ah, those are my tendencies," now I have an entity. So I have to think of it as this combination. The tendencies or thoughts or degrees that in their totality constitute the psychological entity, I conceive of as part of the World-Idea, part of the planetary system; whereas the illuminating light, which has a proclivity towards those tendencies, I think of as belonging to the soul. It's a complex thing I'm thinking of when I'm thinking of the ego.

The first step is that the soul, the embodying soul, thinks it *is* the content. That's the first part. In other words, it first has to say, and think itself, as a body, "I am this."

The embodying soul is identified with a body. This is the beginning of the struggle of the ego. The soul, identified with this body, thinks it is this body, and therefore now identifies itself as the lower self. The struggle begins when it recognizes that it is not this body. Then after that, the soul struggles with that notion that it *is* the lower self. It starts identifying with the higher self. Now, within the ego, there is this struggle between the lower self and that which had a kind of recognition or a notion that it was not this body.

CDA: This identification still remains, even though part of the soul realizes that it's not that.

ANTHONY: Because now the real problem is this constant attempt to identify with the higher and not with the lower. That means you're at the level where you refuse to accept any negative kind of thought and you're always identifying with the more positive kind of thoughts.

KD: The struggle is within the ego? The struggle is between

two parts of the ego, like you've driven a wedge in . . . ?

ANTHONY: Yes, you've driven a wedge in the ego. Now it recognizes that there's a lower part and a higher part to it. That's the pain that the reflective person understands and knows. He would say something like, "I have two souls in my breast." He would start recognizing that struggle within himself. And this is very fierce. It goes on for a long, long time.

FD: I want to distinguish between consciousness and contents, but you seem to be distinguishing between consciousness identified with higher ideas and consciousness identified with lower ideas.

ANTHONY: Yes, but that's not consciousness. We're speaking about the re-embodying soul, whether it identifies with the lower or the higher. I'm not talking about consciousness right now.

FD: Then I'm really confused, because this ray, this embodied soul, if it's of the nature of soul it has to be of the nature of consciousness.

ANTHONY: Fine, but why just consciousness? To me, the embodied soul is of the nature of intelligence. "Consciousness" is too specific a definition. "Intelligence" is much broader. You bring all that you have to bear on what's going on in the psychological personality. I never liked the word "consciousness" because by definition it's undefinable, whereas everybody knows what we mean by intelligence. Even if you try to deny that, you reveal that you understand it.

Read on a little bit more. Read that quote again.

[*Quote is re-read*]

JB: The end of this quote says that the ego is the entity that will win truth and find reality even though in the end it must completely surrender itself. Is there an attainment of truth and reality that's other than the surrender, or are they one thing?

AH: The ego attains its aspiration or enlightenment only through this total renunciation.

ANTHONY: It's a paradox, huh?

AH: It is a paradox. But the way the paradox is articulated for me is: When the ego discovers reality, does it discover the principle of its own reality or an impersonal reality?

ANTHONY: Could we use a different terminology? What is he saying in the simplest way that we can conceive it? Isn't he saying something to the effect that the ego has to develop itself and reach a position of ultimate development before it can become enlightened . . . but once it does become enlightened, in order for it to get enlightened, it, as such, ceases to be?

To understand this quote, I'm saying that you have to take the position that the ego is what is seeking enlightenment, the ego is what has to develop itself to that point where it can be, let's say, the recipient of that enlightenment. And it can be enlightened only after it has surrendered itself.

No ego is going to surrender itself unless it has reached the profoundest level of understanding. That comes either through the satiation of experience or this profundity of understanding, where the ego then realizes that it has to make that effort. And of course, Grace will have to come in to help it, but this is the point we're getting at, all right?

So after that point is reached, when the ego does reach that point, and it's willing to surrender itself and Grace does intervene, then enlightenment occurs. Now, we've got to stop right here, because then if you say, "Who is enlightened?" it is *not* the ego, it is the Void Mind itself that has recognized itself through that ego. But I want to stop right there. You've got to realize the terrible orders he's giving you. I mean, this is an ordeal. The ego has to refine itself. Nobody else is going to do it. No one else is going to teach you. Isn't that the point of the quote?

KD: Does the refinement allow for this self-knowledge to occur? You said you reach the point where the Void Mind recognizes itself.

ANTHONY: I'm sorry I brought that in. Because when you ask the question, "Who is enlightened?" then you bring in the Void Mind. There is no *who* that gets enlightened, because you have to postulate the entitativeness of an ego, and we're not permitted to do that once enlightenment takes place. But who is it that ultimately gets enlightened? It's the Void Mind itself. In other words, it's your own Overself. But how could that get enlightened?

The point I really want to get to here is that you are going to work hard for this. That's the point we want to make sure we understand. The ego's going to have to work for its enlightenment. There are no two ways about it. And then, the paradox is that when it reaches that enlightenment, it can only get enlightened by IT not being. Can't you accept the paradox?

FD: I can get the flavor of it.

ANTHONY: We spoke about paradox last week, that the ego is a paradox. And even when we speak about the soul, that's a paradox, too. On one hand, the soul is of such a nature that it has relationship with nothing—it's utterly Alone, the I AM principle. Then it also has the strange power to project itself forth, and we call that the embodying soul: Through getting embodied in the World-Idea it becomes aware of the nature of the World-Mind. Isn't this a paradox? Can the soul be understood in any other way? You can, of course, believe that the day that the body is created the soul comes with it.

AS: For example, the soul must be both one and many, both divisible and indivisible, as Plotinus says. And I think this is what Plotinus means by a reasoning which is essential to the soul.

ANTHONY: I think the point that Plotinus made was that reasoning is "essential" when it follows the soul. That means it's paradoxical. But if it follows the sensible world, then it's not paradoxical.

So if we go back to the notion of this ego as we understand it, it is of this complex nature. On one hand, it is constituted of all these tendencies—all these ideas which we look upon as belonging to that network of intelligence which is the planetary mind—and it's part of the World-Idea. On the other hand we speak about the soul inhabiting, or working through, such a vehicle. So we've got these two things. This is a paradox. There's no way around it.

LH: Would you say that the ego has to cease, to be? The intelligence, the content, the vehicle, doesn't cease.

ANTHONY: The illumination doesn't cease. But the content can cease. When you understand yourself to be a person who functions in a certain way, you could actually sit down and itemize the different tendencies that constitute your personality. When you go to sleep are they still hanging around?

SA: Yes.

ANTHONY: When you get up in the morning, they'll come into operation, but when you go to sleep you can't say that you're aware of these tendencies, or that you're functioning through these tendencies.

LH: That's true but we're not saying that enlightenment or ceasing of the ego is a state of unconsciousness either, are we?

ANTHONY: No, it's not.

LH: But why did you bring in sleep?

ANTHONY: I just wanted to prove the point that the tendencies are not identical and continuous. They're discontinuous. That which constitutes your ego, as ego, does not have self-identity.

AS: He says near the end of the quote that in order for the enlightenment finally to come there must be this surrender. The embodying soul comes from intelligence, from the soul. If it turns around and surrenders to its Source, dives back into the Source, that which has attached itself to the soul can't stand by itself in that light. It gets cut off.

FD: There's a whole thinning-down process of those

things that cling to that part of the soul, and that's included in refinement of the ego. After that reaches a certain culminating point, then the ego is able to do what you say.

ANTHONY: Which is to surrender its attachment to the lower.

FD: He was saying, turn around and go back to the Source.

ANTHONY: Which would be the same thing. That's the hard part, the surrendering of the attachment to the lower, even if it has been attenuated.

AS: I thought you were suggesting that even the projecting or re-embodying soul itself doesn't have the power to finally accomplish that end. Only surrendering to its own source in the void can finally accomplish that.

ANTHONY: On one hand, the soul, the embodying soul, recognizes its attachment to the lower and tries to surrender it. But it, of its own free will, can't surrender it. The higher power has to come in, and it surrenders. It's this paradoxical nature. When it surrenders, it's no longer ego. It's returning to what it was.

AS: Only that higher soul has the power to finally detach that embodying soul from those tendencies, desires, and so on. Only then can that embodying soul, the light of the soul, finally be fully detached and realize itself, or return to its source.

ANTHONY: And you call that enlightenment. But it's no longer the ego.

The difficulty here is that the illuminating light which has entered into a vehicle and uses that vehicle could be poised in two ways: looking down and identifying with the body or the tendencies, or looking up and identifying with its Source. When it looks down and identifies with the body, we think of it as a refined ego still in the process of making distinctions between various strata, levels, within it. But once that same entity is looking upward, it starts identifying with the Source, and then, let's say, momentarily experiences identification with the Source. We're still talking about a certain person, so for the sake of clarity we say that the ego got enlightened. But by definition you could understand that it isn't the ego that got enlightened, it was the very nature of mind itself that recognizes itself or understands itself.

FD: Now you would be bringing duality into enlightenment.

ANTHONY: Then that could be brought down *into* the ego. That could be brought down into the vehicle, the body.

RG: In that moment, what's added to the mind that is already self-existent?

ANTHONY: Nothing really, except you might say self-recognition or . . .

CDA: What does that mean?

ANTHONY: Self-recognition? It's like going home.

RG: It's self-gnostic, I mean, self-identical.

ANTHONY: "Self-identical" would be better.

RG: That still doesn't elaborate the paradox for me because if it is self-identical, then it's always enlightened.

ANTHONY: Yes, but that's so.

RG: If it's always enlightened, then what does it care?

ANTHONY: You say, "What does it care?" and we'll be back into trouble again. It's got to care. It's got to see that it has a role to fulfill in the world, as part of the World-Idea.

RG: The soul itself, and that's through the ego.

ANTHONY: As we pointed out, how could it become acquainted or participate in the World-Idea except through the body that it must use? What's going to become part of the World-Idea, an infinite part of the World-Idea?

RG: So it is the ego that gets enlightened? Because what else needs to get enlightened?

ANTHONY: OK, there's no harm in saying that. Because the ego that gets enlightened knows that it is, so to speak, being and not ego-being. So it's all right.

RG: Would you say that the being that gets enlightened has become a perfected vehicle for revelation of the soul?

ANTHONY: I don't think so. I think it's just starting. And you know, from what we've heard of people like the Buddha, it's a long, long development. It goes on for many, many millenia.

NOTES

1. Reference is to the quote: "A master counselled patience. 'Can you break iron with your hands?' he asked. 'File it down little by little and one day you will be able to snap it into two pieces with a single effort. So it is with the ego.' " (v6, 8:4.195)

2. For a detailed exposition and comparison of the Long Path and the Short Path—and which schools emphasize each approach—see *The Notebooks of Paul Brunton*, volume 15, part 1 (chapters 1, 2, 4, 5) and volume 3, part 1, chapter 1.

3. Hindu philosophy speaks of four states of consciousness: *vaishwanara* (waking), *taijasa* (dream or creative), *prajna* (sleep or wisdom), and *turiya* (unconditioned).

4. A paraphrase of Plotinus, *Ennead* VI.5.7: "To know without image is to be." (MacKenna translation)

5. Note the shift from describing the ego's source as "mistaken thought" to Source as higher self.

6. A paraphrase of Proverbs 23:7.

CODA

☐

WHAT IS THE USE, ask many questioners, of first, an evolution of the human soul which merely brings it back to the same point where it started and second, of developing a selfhood through the long cycles of evolution only to have it merged or dissolved in the end into the unselfed Absolute? Is not the whole scheme absurdly useless? The answer is that if this were really the case, the criticism passed would be quite a fair one. But it is not the case. The unit of life emanated from the Overself begins with the merest glimmer of consciousness, appearing on our plane as a protozoic cell. It evolves eventually into the fullest human consciousness, including the intellectual and spiritual. It does not finish as it began; on the contrary, there is a grand purpose behind all its travail. There is thus a wide gulf between its original state and its final one. The second point is more difficult to clear up, but it may be plainly affirmed that man's individuality survives even in the divinest state accessible to him. There it becomes the same in quality but not identical in essence. The most intimate mental and physical experiences of human love cast a little light for our comprehension of this mystery. The misunderstanding which leads to these questions arises chiefly because of the error which believes that it is the divine soul which goes through all this pilgrimage by reincarnating in a series of earthly forms.

The true teaching about reincarnation is not that the divine soul enters into the captivity and ignorance of the flesh again and again but that something emanated from the soul, that is, a unit of life that eventually develops into the personal ego, does so. The Overself contains this reincarnating ego within itself but does not itself reincarnate. It is the parent; the ego is only its offspring. The long and tremendous evolution through which the unit of life passes from its primitive cellular existence to its matured human one is a genuine evolution of its consciousness. Whoever believes that the process first plunges a soul down from the heights into a body or forces Spirit to lose itself in Matter, and then leaves it no alternative but to climb all the way back to the lost summit again, believes wrongly. The Overself never descends or climbs, never loses its own sublime consciousness. What really does this is something that emanates from it and that consequently holds its capacity and power in latency, something which is finited out of the Overself's infinitude and becomes first, the simple unit of life and later, the complex human ego. It is not the Overself that suffers and struggles during this long unfoldment but its child, the ego. It is not the Overself that slowly expands its intelligence and consciousness, but the ego. It is not the Overself that gets deluded by ignorance and passion, by selfishness and extroversion, but the ego.

The belief in the merger of the ego held by some Hindu sects or in its annihilation held by some Buddhist ones, is unphilosophical. The "I" differentiated itself out of the infinite ocean of Mind into a distinct individuality after a long development through the diverse kingdoms of Nature. Having thus arrived at consciousness of what it is, having travelled the spiral of growth from germ to man, the result of all this effort is certainly not gained only to be thrown away.

Were this to happen then the entire history of the human race would be a meaningless one, its entire travail a resultless one, its entire aspiration a valueless one. If evolution were merely the complementary return journey of an involutionary process, if the evolving entity arrived only at its starting point for all its pains, then the whole plan would be a senseless one. If the journey of man consisted of nothing more than treading a circle from the time of his emergence from the Divine Essence to the time of his mergence back into it, it would be a vain and useless activity. It would be a stupendous adventure but also a stupid one. There is something more than that in his movement. Except in the speculations of certain theorists, it simply does not happen.

The self-consciousness thus developed will not be dissolved, extinguished, or re-absorbed into the Whole again, leaving not a trace behind. Rather will it begin a new spiral of evolution towards higher altitudes of consciousness and diviner levels of being, in which it will co-operate as harmoniously with the universal existence as formerly it collided against it. It will not separate its own good from the general good. Here is part of the answer to this question: What are the ultimate reasons for human wanderings through the world-process? That life matters, that the universe possesses meaning, and that the evolutionary agonies are leading to something worthwhile—these are beliefs we are entitled to hold. If the cosmos is a wheel which turns and turns endlessly, it does not turn aimlessly. Evolution does not return us to the starting point as we were. The ascent is not a circle but a spiral.

Evolution presupposes that its own possibility has always been latent within the evolving entities. Hence the highest form is hidden away in the lowest one. There is development from the blindly instinctive life of animals to the consciously thinking life of man. The blind instinctive struggles of the plant to sustain itself are displaced in the evolutionary process by the intelligent self-conscious efforts of the man. Nor does this ascent end in the Vedantic merger or the Buddhistic annihilation. It could not, for it is a development of the individuality. Everywhere we find that evolution produces variety. There are myriads of individual entities, but each possesses some quality of uniqueness which distinguishes it from all others. Life may be one but its multitudinous expressions do differ, as though difference were inherent in such expression.

Evolution as mentalistically defined by philosophy is not quite the same as evolution as materialistically defined by Darwin. With us it is simply the mode of striving, through rhythmic rise and fall, for an ever fuller expansion of the individual unit's consciousness. However, the ego already possesses all such possibilities latently. Consequently the whole process, although apparently an ascending one, is really an unfolding one.

(v16, 26:4.257 AND *Perspectives*, P. 368)

INDEX

OTHER TITLES OF RELATED INTEREST FROM

)n

FOR ADDITIONAL INFORMATION, to receive a free catalog offering many other books, audio- and videotapes, or to place an order, please write Larson Publications, 4936 State Route 414, Burdett, New York 14818 or call 607-546-9342 between 9 a.m. and 5 p.m. Eastern time.